THE CASE FOR CHRISTIANITY

ST JUSTIN MARTYR'S ARGUMENTS FOR RELIGIOUS LIBERTY AND JUDICIAL JUSTICE

ROBERT M. HADDAD

Published by Taylor Trade Publishing
An imprint of The Rowman & Littlefield Publishing Group, Inc.
4501 Forbes Boulevard, Suite 200, Lanham, Maryland 20706
http://www.rlpgtrade.com

Estover Road, Plymouth PL6 7PY, United Kingdom

Distributed by National Book Network

British Library Cataloguing in Publication Information Available

ISBN 978-1-58979-575-4 (paperback)
ISBN 978-1-58979-584-6 (electronic)

To my wife, Suzi,
who has patiently supported me throughout the years of
my studies.

Contents

Preface

Why is reading about St Justin of Neapolis, a saint and martyr of the second century AD, important for Christians of the twenty-first century?

St Justin lived during times similar to our own in many ways. Rome was the dominant world power and appeared for all intents and purposes unassailable. Economically, militarily and geographically Rome was at its height. Yet, it was beset by a number of growing problems—moral decay, family breakdown, falling birth rates, just to name a few. Religiously, Rome was conservative, yet eastern religions and mystery cults were spreading westwards and gaining many adherents. Fidelity to the gods was seen as essential to Rome's continued prosperity and survival. Failure to render the gods their due threatened to bring down their wrath and despoil the empire.

Hence, the problem of the Christians. They refused to give any acknowledgement to the Graeco-Roman pantheon, and thus were considered as dangerous and impious atheists. For Rome's survival, they therefore needed to be eliminated. In their efforts to destroy Christianity the Roman judicial procedure was arbitrary and ruthless. All that was needed for summary execution was the admission of bearing the Christian name and refusing to sacrifice to the Graeco-Roman gods.

St Justin's efforts were urgent and heroic. He petitioned the very authority that persecuted Christians with a series of arguments pleading for judicial justice and religious liberty. His arguments appealed to the nobler sense in Romans, as well as to common sense. At the same time they contained an 'evangelistic edge' that sought his readers' conversion to Christianity. This spirit of evangelism is very pronounced in St Justin's other great work, Dialogue with Trypho the Jew.

In a number of respects the plight of second century Christians reflects the suffering of Christians in various modern-day contexts. St Justin's arguments are, therefore, of a nature that can be appreciated by many a modern reader and should be of interest and relevance to Christians deprived of religious liberty today. St Justin's struggle also reminds us that we in the West who enjoy religious freedom should never take it for granted.

Robert M. Haddad, 2009

Chapter 1

Introduction

"Christianos ad leonem!"—Christians to the lion! These words were written in reference to the arbitrary justice meted out against Christians during the late second century AD.[1] From the reign of the Emperor Nero (AD 54-68), Christianity was regarded with suspicion and hatred by both the Roman authorities and the general populace. At first, the charge against Christians was "incendiarism"; very quickly it became "hatred of the human race" (*odium generis humani*), according to Tacitus.[2] Throughout the second century, Christians were also subject to a chorus of accusations and calumnies—believed both by many indifferent and avowedly hostile non-Christians—that they were atheists who practised sexual licentiousness, child murder and cannibalism.[3] To vindicate Christianity against its accusers and persecutors Christians had to develop many varied arguments to explain and defend their beliefs and practices.

Furthermore, to attract converts from among the peoples in the wider expanse of the Graeco-Roman world it was necessary to do more than simply quote passages and prophecies from

1 Tertullian, *Apology* 40.2 (AD 197). All quotes from Tertullian's works are taken from *Ante Nicene Fathers*, vol. 3, ed. Alexander Roberts and James Donaldson, rev. A. Cleveland Coxe, Eerdmans, Grand Rapids, 1897.

2 Tacitus, *Annals* 15.44.

3 L. W. Barnard, *St. Justin Martyr: The First and Second Apologies*, Paulist Press, New York/Mahwah N.J., 1997, p. 1; cf. Minucius Felix, *Octavius* 9 (inter AD 218-235) ACW (*Ancient Christian Writers*) 56.

the Hebrew scriptures and proclaim their fulfilment in Jesus of Nazareth. To meet these challenges emerged the Apologists. They introduced into post-apostolic literature the spirit of apology found in apostolic writings such as Luke-Acts with a view to providing reasoned replies to the questions being asked by the outside world.[4]

The earliest Christian apologists appeared during the reign of the emperor Hadrian (AD 117-138) and in their 'classical' phase lasted until the reign of Commodus (AD 180-192), hence coinciding with the 'brilliant period of Roman life.' A Greek named Quadratus composed the first known apology in defence of Christianity and presented it to Hadrian during the latter's visit to Athens in AD 125.[5] Aristides of Athens, who addressed his "apology for the faith" most probably to the emperor Antoninus between AD 140-145, followed him. The suggested occasion for this apology was the charge of sexual immorality made by the famous rhetorician Fronto.[6] In subsequent decades appeared Apollinaris of Laodicea,[7] Melito of Sardis,[8] Tatian the Syrian,[9] Athenagoras of Athens[10] and Miltiades,[11] all responding

---

4 E. F. Osborn, *Justin Martyr*, J. C. B. Mohr, Tübingen, 1973, p. 14.

5 Entitled *On Behalf of our Religion*, the only extant fragment of this apology is preserved in Eusebius, *History of the Church*, 4.3.2 and asserts that the miracles of Jesus were authentic and witnessed by numerous people.

6 R. M. Grant, "The Chronology of the Greek Apologists," *Vigiliae Christianae* 9 (1955), pp. 25-33 at p. 25.

7 Apollinaris addressed his apology, *On behalf of the Faith*, to the emperor Marcus Aurelius shortly after AD 174 (Eusebius, *History of the Church*, 5.5.4).

8 Though entitled *To Antoninus*, Melito wrote to Marcus Aurelius to complain about the "new decrees" which led to confiscation of Christian property and inflicted death (Grant, "The Chronology of the Greek Apologists," p. 27).

9 Tatian addressed his apology "to the Greeks" after AD 176. According to Grant, "The Chronology of the Greek Apologists," p. 28, "Tatian's treatise is positively disloyal and cannot have failed to impress Rome unfavourably."

10 Athenagoras addressed his apology, *Supplication for the Christians*, to the emperors Marcus Aurelius and Lucius Aurelius Commodus shortly after AD 176. It contains a reaffirmation of Christian loyalty towards the empire.

11 Miltiades wrote three treatises during the reign of Marcus Aurelius Antonius and Lucius Aurelius Commodus entitled *Against the Greeks, Against the Jews,* and *To the Cosmic Rulers* (Eusebius, *History of the Church*, 5.17.5).

to the severe persecution of AD 176-180. Another apologist of the time, Theophilus of Antioch, wrote three books to a high-ranking official in the last phases of this persecution.[12] Justin appeared and wrote in the midst of these men between AD 140 and 165.[13]

Justin Martyr was born somewhere between AD 100-110 in Flavia Neapolis in Samaria, of Graeco-Roman immigrants. Flavia Neapolis was founded by the Emperor Vespasian (AD 69-79) as a Roman colony near the ancient city of Sichem in Samaria. Justin on one occasion called himself a Samaritan (*Dial.* 120). A philosopher at heart, Justin passed through various Greek philosophical schools (Stoic, Peripatetic, Pythagorean, Middle-Platonic) before his conversion to Christianity around the year AD 130 at the age of thirty, during the reign of Emperor Hadrian (*Dial.* 2). Arising from his 'journey' Justin saw that "Christian philosophy alone was safe and useful" (*Dial.* 8).[14] Justin later came to Rome around AD 150 where he founded his school of Christian philosophy and entered into active controversy with the attacks against Christianity. According to Eusebius[15], Justin was prepared to risk failure and even death to

12 Theophilus in *To Autolycus* "insists on Christian loyalty to the emperor, as emperor but not as God, and provides a chronological sketch of Roman history" (Grant, "The Chronology of the Greek Apologists," p. 30).

13 Justin wrote his *Apologies* between 148 and 155 AD; The *Dialogue with Trypho the Jew* was written circa 155 AD. See, Rev. William A. Jurgens, *The Faith of the Early Fathers*, The Liturgical Press, Collegeville, Minnesota, 1970, Vol. 1, pp. 50, 57, 58.

14 As to Justin's philosophical journey, Barnard, *St. Justin Martyr*, p. 11, states, "(h)is was a typical experience born of the eclecticism of the age. Pupils, in those days, passed from teacher to teacher in their search for philosophical truth almost as a matter of course." J.C.M. van Winden, *An Early Christian Philosopher: Justin Martyr's Dialogue with Trypho Chapters One to Nine*, E.J. Brill, Leiden, 1971, pp. 17 and 126, terms this journey Justin's "ascent through Greek philosophy," rediscovering the "primordial philosophy" originally sent down by God and now embodied in Christianity. According to J. J. Sikora, "Philosophy and Christian Wisdom According to Saint Justin Martyr," *Franciscan Studies* 23/1 (1963-4), pp. 244-256 at p. 248, Justin is a philosopher for "he is a man wholly committed to the truth and to living according to the truth."

15 Eusebius, *History of the Church* 4.11.8, speaks of Justin thus: "Justin was the most active; wearing the garb of a philosopher he proclaimed the divine message, and contended by means of his writings on behalf of the Faith."

defend the Christian faith. This he achieved together with six of his students (namely Chariton, Charito, Euelpistus, Hierax, Paeon, Liberianus) at the order of the Roman Prefect Junius Rusticus, during the reign of Marcus Aurelius, somewhere between AD 163 and 167[16], probably as a result of a conflict with the Cynic philosopher Crescens (*2 Apol.* 3). Three versions of his *Martyrum S. Justini et Sociorum*, embodying a reliable third-century tradition, are extant.[17]

As an apologist, Justin was a successful innovator (and in the process he touched on most of Christian theology)—so much so that all his successors, including Irenaeus, Tertullian and the Alexandrians, adopted and developed his ideas.[18] Justin was Irenaeus' favourite apologist.[19] In the opinion of Cruttwell[20], Tertullian took from Justin his most effective weapon—that of retorting the opponent's charges upon himself. According to von Campenhausen[21], "nearly all the Greek Fathers of the Church were, consciously or unconsciously, his imitators," anticipating more or less the arguments later used by other Church Fathers and even the mediaeval polemicists.[22] Barnard puts it well in these words: "What Justin accomplished in the second century

16 P. Keresztes, "The So-called Second Apology of Justin," *Latomus* 24 (1965), pp. 858-869 at p. 869.

17 Barnard, *St. Justin Martyr*, pp. 6 and 97. The *Acta* are reproduced in H. Musurillo, *The Acts of the Christian Martyrs*, Clarendon Press, Oxford, 1972, pp. 42-61.

18 W. H. Wagner, *Christianity in the Second Century: After the Apostles*, Fortress Press, Minneapolis, 1994, p. 159; T. Stylianopoulos, "Justin Martyr," in *Encyclopedia of Early Christianity*, E. Ferguson, ed., Garland Publishing, New York & London, 1997, pp. 647-650 at p. 648.

19 R. M. Grant, *Greek Apologists of the Second Century*, SCM Press, London, 1988, p. 61.

20 C. T. Cruttwell, *A Literary History of Early Christianity*, vol. 2, C. Griffin & Co., London, 1893, p. 335.

21 H. von Campenhausen, *The Fathers of the Greek Church*, A & C Black, London, 1963, p. 15.

22 S. Krauss & W. Horbury, *The Jewish-Christian Controversy from the Earliest Times to 1789*, vol. 1, J. C. B. Mohr, Tübingen, 1996, p. 30.

was the seedbed of the later Church."[23]

Of Justin's many writings only three have survived substantially intact: his two *Apologies* to the Emperor Antoninus Pius, his sons and to the Roman Senate, and the *Dialogue with Trypho the Jew*, addressed to a certain Marcus Pompeius. These survive in a single manuscript of poor quality copied in the fourteenth century.[24] Four small fragments contained in the works of other writers are also considered genuine. Justin's lost treatise on heresies (*Syntagma*) became a model for other authors and Eusebius[25] credited him with five other works: *Discourse to the Greeks*, *Admonition to the Greeks*, *On the Divine Monarchy*, *Psalmist* and *On the Soul*. Barnard[26] lists the following as belonging to the pseudo-Justinian corpus: (a) *Address to the Greeks*; (b) *Hortatory Address to the Greeks*; (c) *On the Unity of God*; (d) *A Fragment on the Resurrection*; (e) *Exposition of the True Faith*; (f) *Letter to Zenas and Serenus*; (g) *Refutation of certain Aristotelian Doctrines*; (h) *Questions and Answers to the Orthodox*; (i) *Christian Questions asked to the Greeks*.

The purpose of this work is to present and analyse Justin's apologetical arguments as contained in his genuine works, namely *First* and *Second Apologies* and *Dialogue with Trypho the Jew*, in response to the so-called "five-fold attack"[27] launched against Christianity in the second century AD by the Roman state, philosophers, the general public (popular calumnies),

---

23 Barnard, *St. Justin Martyr*, p. 21.

24 J. Quasten, *Patrology*, vol. 1: *The Beginnings of Patristic Literature*, Newman Press, Maryland, 1950, p. 197. H. Chadwick, "Justin Martyr's Defence of Christianity," *Bulletin of the John Rylands Library* 47 (1965), pp. 275-297 at p. 275, laments this fact, stating, "as a result of its corruptions we cannot be completely sure of Justin's opinion on all points."

25 Eusebius, *History of the Church* 4.18.

26 L. W. Barnard, *Justin Martyr: His Life and Thought*, Cambridge University Press, London, 1967, p. 172.

27 E. F. Osborn, "Justin's Response to Second Century Challenges," *Australian Biblical Review* 14 (1966), pp. 37-54 at p. 54.

heretics and the Jews. Were Justin's arguments appropriate taking into account the rhetorical and literary conventions of second-century Graeco-Roman culture, the contemporary social situation, Justin's intended audience and his purpose?

In summary, Justin intended his *Apologies* to be published as open letters to the government seeking the following: (i) an end to the arbitrary injustices committed by the Roman judicial procedure against Christians by establishing the latter's innocence in the eyes of the general public and philosophically-minded (and through them to the emperors) against the charges of atheism, immorality and disloyalty; (ii) to overcome ignorance and prejudice by showing forth Christianity's rationality through an unabridged presentation of Christian doctrines and practices, and to recommend it to his pagan addressees as the only safe and useful philosophy so to ultimately win their adherence; and (iii) for the catechetical, rhetorical and apologetical formation of Christians already in the Church. However, Justin's hope of getting the emperors to repeal the anti-Christian laws was not ultimately realised.

Justin intended *Dialogue* to be read by unattached Gentiles, as well as Christians already within the fold, for the purposes of converting the former to Christianity, to provide a helpful internal sourcebook for study by Christians to defend their beliefs against well-educated Jews and to convert as many of them as possible, to combat Judaising Christians who wished to foist law-keeping on Gentile Christians in Rome, and to counter Marcion and his rejection of the Torah.

Apologetics has always been a part of the life and mission of the Church. We read in the Acts of the Apostles how St. Paul, while in Rome, received people "… at his lodgings in great numbers. From morning until evening he explained the matter to them, testifying to the kingdom of God and trying to convince them about Jesus both from the law of Moses and from the prophets" (Acts 28:23). Justin inherited this spirit and blended it with his knowledge of philosophy to contend with a Graeco-Roman world that, a century after Paul, was more aware of and hostile to Christianity. Justin provides the earliest example of how apologists must adapt their methods and arguments to deal with the particular circumstances and challenges of the age.

Chapter 2

The Factors that Inspired the Apologetical Works of Justin

Justin lived during the second century AD, a century described by Edward Gibbon as the "most happy and prosperous" for the human race.[1] This happiness and prosperity, however, did not extend to the Christians. The attacks on Christianity made the position of Christians both confused and precarious. Justin claimed to witness the treatment of Christians first-hand (*1 Apol.* 1) and denounced particular judicial actions against them as arbitrary and unjust (*2 Apol.* 1, 2). While living and teaching in Rome, Justin encountered critical philosophical and intellectual attacks, particularly from the Cynic Crescens (*2 Apol.* 3). He witnessed the confusion and divisions caused by heretics and protested the honours and freedom he supposed the state afforded them (*1 Apol.* 26). Justin was also cognisant of so-called Jewish "cursing" of Christians in synagogues (*Dial.* 133) and what he believed were "slanders" spread by emissaries

---

1 E. Gibbon, *History of the Decline and Fall of the Roman Empire*, ch. 3, J. M. Dent & Sons, London, 1966.

throughout the empire (*Dial.* 17). Finally, Justin engaged a fifth front, viz., the popular calumnies spread against Christians by the general population (*2 Apol.* 13).

The wide range of opposition to Christianity demanded a wide range of responses. However, Christians for the most part were a simple and unlettered people and few possessed the literary skills to provide the necessary answers. Justin was an exception and he felt compelled to take up the defence on behalf of the Church: "O Romans, what has recently happened in your city under Urbicus, and what is likewise being done everywhere by the governors unreasonably, have compelled me to compose these arguments for your sakes" (*2 Apol.* 1). Together, Justin's writings would ultimately engage all aspects of the 'five-fold attack,'using rhetoric and philosophy with outside analysts and internal questioners, signalling that Christians were sufficiently cultured to be treated at least with respect. "Speculative thought and Christian philosophy began with Justin."[2]

It is the purpose of this chapter to analyse in detail the particular 'attacks' that raged against Christianity during Justin's time. As just stated, Justin himself either personally experienced or was aware of these attacks. An appreciation of the second-century threats to Christianity supplies us with both an understanding of what motivated Justin to write and what he hoped to achieve through his works.

---

2 Barnard, *St. Justin Martyr*, p. 26. According to Barnard, p. 12, theology and philosophy in the mind of Justin formed but one wisdom, which was fully revealed through Jesus Christ. This did not amount to a break with Greek philosophy, rather, the truths in Greek philosophy, especially Platonism, were a preparation for the Gospel. Contrast this view with that of the Apostle Paul, who associates philosophy with empty deceit and a potential source of peril for Christians (Col. 2:8). Contrary to Barnard, O. Skarsaune, "The Conversion of Justin Martyr," *Studia Theologica* 30 (1976), pp. 53-73 at p. 56, states, "There is no smooth passage from Plato to Christ in Justin's story ... It is not Platonism itself but its destruction that prepares Justin for conversion." Stylianopoulos, "Justin Martyr," p. 649, notes that while Platonic influence is unmistakable, Justin in his writings still sits in judgement on philosophy and is no uncritical advocate.

(1) The State

The most obvious attack on Christianity came from the various branches of the Roman imperial government. Early in *1 Apology*, Justin censures Roman judicial procedure, accusing it of condemning Christians simply for their name (*nomen Christianum*), without any other crime (*flagitia*) being proved against them (*1 Apol.* 4, 7, 8; cf. *2 Apol.* 2).

The legal basis for the persecution of Christians during the second century remains unclear. Vague references to a *lex* against Christians (such as Athenagoras' *Legatio* 7; Tertullian's *Apol.* 4.4ff.) show merely that Christianity was illegal, not how it came to be so. Keresztes[3] argues that a new law was specifically enacted by Nero to scapegoat and eliminate the hated sect. Others have maintained that already existing criminal laws of Caesar and Augustus against unauthorised associations (*collegia illicita*) were simply extended to include Christians.[4] Still others assert that second-century Christians were merely subject to the general coercive powers of the magistrates, taking the Neronian punishments as a sufficient precedent.[5] Most probably, prefects or provincial governors punished Christians for repudiating the *mos maiorum*, or ancestral traditions, the unwritten code of laws and conduct accumulated over the centuries that institutionalised Roman cultural traditions, societal mores, and general policies, without recourse to any specific law passed by the Senate or the emperor. As Barnes[6] notes, "It is in the minds of men, not in

---

3 P. Keresztes, "The Literary Genre of Justin's First Apology," *Vigiliae Christianae* 19 (1965), pp. 99-110 at p. 106.
4 M. Cary, *A History of Rome Down to the Reign of Constantine*, 2ⁿᵈ edn, MacMillan, London, 1965, p. 766; A. N. Sherwin-White, "The Early Persecutions and Roman Law Again," *Journal of Theological Studies* n.s. 3 (1952-1953), pp. 199-213.
5 L. Hertling and E. Kirschbaum, *The Roman Catacombs and their Martyrs*, Darton, Longman & Todd, London, 1960, p. 121.
6 T. D. Barnes, *Early Christianity in the Roman Empire*, Variorum Reprints, London, 1984, p. 50.

the demands of Roman law, that the roots of the persecution of the Christians in the Roman Empire are to be sought."

From the perspective of the Roman state, Christianity was a "new-fangled cult"[7] that "fled the light and conspired in the shadows" (*latebrosa et lucifuga natio*).[8] It was accused of attracting converts from the ignorant and the lower classes and of worshipping a convicted felon in the place of the traditional gods and the emperor.[9] Justin himself readily admitted that Christians refused honour and sacrifices to "such deities as human beings have made" (*1 Apol.* 9; cf. *1 Apol.* 29). Conversions to Christianity threatened to subvert the established order of society as such not only involved a change of belief but effected a radical transformation in which past religious affiliations were rejected in favour of a new and alien identity with its own interpretation of the past and present. The danger to the state appeared even more ominous by the tenacity and universality of the Christian mission that sought to convert to its ranks all and sundry without exception.

The Christian rejection of traditional Graeco-Roman religion amounted to impiety, or atheism, and endangered the *pax deorum*, for it risked provoking the wrath of the gods on whose goodwill the prosperity of the state was believed to depend.[10] This was certainly the concern of the emperor Domitian (AD 81-96), whose authoritative style and enforcement of the emperor-

---

7 W. H. C. Frend, *The Rise of Christianity*, Darton, Longman and Todd, London, 1984, p. 177.

8 Minucius Felix, *Octavius* 8.4, quoting Q. Caecilius Natalis.

9 The Romans termed rejection of the emperor-cult as the treasonable crime of *maiestas*. The philosopher Celsus (c. AD 180) alleged that "the Christians entered into secret associations with each other contrary to law ... [and] the 'love-feasts' of the Christians ... had their origin in the common danger": In Origen, *Against Celsus*, 1.1, c. AD 248.

10 G. E. M. de St. Croix, "The Persecutions," in *The Crucible of Christianity*, A. Toynbee, ed., Thames and Hudson, London, 1969, pp. 331-351, at p. 347; E. Pagels, "Christian Apologists and the 'Fall of the Angels': An Attack on Roman Imperial Power," *Harvard Theological Review* 78 (1985), pp. 301-325 at p. 314.

cult claimed a number of victims of high rank on charges of "atheism" and "slipping into Jewish customs."[11]

Trajan's rescript to the governor of Bithynia and Pontus, Pliny the Younger (AD 111-112), showed that admission of being Christian, together with refusal to worship the state Gods and the emperor, implied subversive tendencies and/or hostility to the state. The governor was expected to put suspects on trial where there were formal accusations and persuade them to revile Christ and perform an act of sacrifice, or burn incense before the emperor's statue, as proof that they were not Christians.[12] Impenitent Christians were to be punished, even with death. Proof of crimes against other laws was not required.[13] But Trajan discouraged active persecution, special investigations, or 'witch-hunts' (*conquirendi non sunt*) and forbad the following up of anonymous denunciations as "both bad practice and contrary to the spirit of our times" (*nam et pessimi exempli nec saeculi est*). However, it was still possible for those so determined to harass Christians arbitrarily.[14]

It is uncertain whether Trajan's reply made a change in the legal position of Christians or was the reaffirmation of an already established principle. Trajan's immediate successor, Hadrian, in his rescript of AD 124-125 to Minucius Fundanus,

11 Dio Cassius 67.14.1-2. M. P. Charlesworth, "Some Observations on Ruler-Cult Especially in Rome," *Harvard Theological Review* 28 (1935), pp. 31-42 at p. 32, speculates that the practice of making offerings before a statue of the emperor and swearing by his "genius" (*"genius sacratissimi imperatoris Domitiani"*) as a test of religious conformity and loyalty may have begun with Domitian. That Christian and not Jewish converts were the intended targets is demonstrated by the fact that the Roman Jewish community as a whole was left undisturbed and that no Jews were banished from Rome: K. P. Donfried and P. Richardson, *Judaism and Christianity in First Century Rome*, W.B. Eerdmans, Grand Rapids, Michigan, 1998, p. 107.

12 W. H. C. Frend, *The Early Church – From the beginnings to 461*, 3rd edn, SCM Press, London, 1991, pp. 45-46.

13 Pliny, *Epistle* 10.97.1-2; K. Baus, *Handbook of Church History*, vol. 1: *From the Apostolic Community to Constantine*, Burns & Oates, London, 1965, p. 134.

14 P. Keresztes, "Law and Arbitrariness in the Persecution of the Christians and Justin's First Apology," *Vigiliae Christianae* 18 (1964), pp. 204-214 at p. 207.

proconsul of Asia, prohibited condemnation in response to "noisy demands and shouts" or formless general denunciations made by tumultuous mobs. Hadrian ordained that proceedings could only be instituted if an accusation was brought in correct form before a court and that an accused ought to be condemned solely when they "broke the law." Only then was the governor to pronounce sentence "according to the gravity of the crime." Those bringing false or frivolous allegations of Christianity were to be severely punished for *calumnia*.[15]

Opinions conflict as to whether Hadrian's rescript differs in effect from Trajan's or simply reaffirms the norms laid down by the latter. Hadrian's reply seems to presuppose that there had been an outcry against *delatores* employing the imputation of Christianity to arouse prejudice against those whom they had accused of less serious crimes. Frend[16] and Baus[17] argue in favour of relief for the Christians, while Moreau[18] argues that Hadrian's rescript was nothing more than a reaffirmation of the Trajanic norms. Justin certainly saw it as providing relief for Christians (*1 Apol.* 68) and there is every indication that the situation for Christians during Hadrian's reign was substantially ameliorated.[19] Barnes[20] holds that Hadrian was in fact only concerned with those who were falsely accused of Christianity. Whatever the case, Hadrian's rescript only provided guidance to a particular proconsul as to how to act in his own province. In other provinces, and in subsequent decades, it was still open to governors and authorities to follow the maxim that the *nomen*

---

15 The full text of Hadrian's rescript is reproduced by Justin in *1 Apol.* 68.5-10. See also Eusebius, *History of the Church* 4.9.

16 Frend, *The Early Church*, p. 47.

17 Baus, *Handbook of Church History*, p. 135.

18 J. Moreau, *The Persecution of Christians in the Roman Empire*, Presses Universitaires de France, Paris, 1956, pp. 15-19.

19 Besides the execution of the Bishop of Rome, Telesphorus, no executions of Christians in any part of the empire can be attributed with certainty to the reign of Hadrian: Baus, *Handbook of Church History*, p. 136; Frend, *The Early Church*, 58.

20 Barnes, *Early Christianity*, p. 37.

Christianum was sufficient for punishment. This is evidenced by Justin's account—contained in *2 Apol.* 1-2—of the three Christians martyred in Rome who were executed by Q. Lollius Urbicus because of their steadfast profession of faith.[21]

Antoninus Pius continued to protect Christians from mob accusation, but this protection was not universally effective.[22] Marcus Aurelius (AD 161-80) personally disliked Christians for what he believed to be their stubbornness in favour of an illusion,[23] but made no change to the moderate policy against Christianity, as is evidenced from his rescript to the governor of Lyons in AD 177.[24] However, he did insist more than the others upon the performance of the state cults and amended administrative procedures to make denunciation of Christians easier.

(2) The Philosophers

A philosopher himself, Justin had a special admiration for pagan philosophers who, through human reason, discovered and expressed truth well. Socrates was an example of such a philosopher (*2 Apol.* 10). Nevertheless, it was second-century philosophy, with its decadence and contradictions,[25] which in

21 One of the accused, Ptolemy, was asked by Urbicus only one question: "Are you a Christian?" Receiving an affirmative answer, Urbicus pronounced the death sentence. The trial of St Polycarp of Smyrna (inter AD 155-157) also shows the very characteristics Hadrian's rescript decades earlier meant to rectify. See Grant, *Greek Apologists*, p. 45.
22 Osborn, *Justin Martyr*, p. 2. Near the end of his reign, Antoninus intervened to stop persecution of Christians in Asia and Greece: A. W. F. Blunt, *The Apologies of Justin Martyr*, Cambridge University Press, London, 1911, p. xviii. Also, according to Grant, *Greek Apologists*, p. 45, no Roman bishop was a martyr under the Antonines.
23 Marcus Aurelius, *Meditations* 3.16; 11.3. Marcus also had as advisers Fronto and Rusticus, both hostile to Christianity: Osborn, *Justin Martyr*, p. 2.
24 Eusebius, *History of the Church* 5.1.47.
25 The satirist Lucian of Samosata in his *Fugitivi* bewails the decadence of philosophy (3 and 12). In his *Hermotimus*, Lucian attacks the contradictions in philosophy (27), as well as the stubbornness and shortcuts of philosophers (51). Justin viewed philosophical contradiction as a consequence of not knowing Christ "for He was and is the logos who is in every person" (*2 Apol.* 10).

the opinion of one scholar comprised Christianity's "most serious opponent."[26] The dominant philosophy of Justin's time was Stoicism, to which the Antonine emperors faithfully adhered. Other philosophies of importance included Platonism, Middle Platonism, Cynicism, and Epicureanism.[27] The majority of their leading proponents—including Plutarch, Epictetus, Celsus, Numenius of Apamea, Maximus of Tyre, Artemidorus of Daldis, Aelius Aristides and Galen—accepted the religion of the traditional gods, and some of these men directed all the subtlety and skill of classical antiquity against Christianity on the grounds that it offended the *mos maiorum*.[28]

Justin disputed directly with the Cynic Crescens, who proclaimed that the Christians were "godless and impious" (*2 Apol.* 3). Pagans who were better informed made more specific attacks, starting with attacks against Christ's uniqueness. As H. Chadwick reconstructs, "Why should the Christians suppose that the healing wonders of Christ are superior to those of Asclepius? Is not the idea of the virgin birth analogous to the birth of Perseus?"[29] In addition, specific articles of the Christian belief, particularly the doctrines of creation, revelation, angels, judgement, hell, the resurrection, human freedom and responsibility, were all opposed through reasoned argument.

Speeches, pamphlets and books became the vehicles of

---

26 C.C. Martindale, *St. Justin the Martyr*, Harding & More, London, 1921, p. 24.

27 The contemporary philosophy of the educated, however, was not limited to a single school of thought. As H. Chadwick, *Early Christian Thought and the Classical Tradition: Studies in Justin, Clement, and Origen*, Clarendon Press, Oxford, 1966, pp. 5-6, notes, "[t]he diffused popular philosophy … (was) … without specialist responsibility or knowledge, as the source of their guiding principles was an eclectic affair, not bound within either the straitjacket of school orthodoxy or the requirements of rigid internal consistency."

28 Though there was not a great fondness for the Jews either, they were at least regarded as a distinct people with a traditional religion that was ancient. See H. Remus, "Justin Martyr's Argument with Judaism," in *Anti-Judaism in Early Christianity*, vol. 2: *Separation and Polemic*, S. G. Wilson, ed., Wilfrid Laurier University Press, Waterloo, Ontario, 1986, pp. 59-80 at p. 79.

29 Chadwick, "Justin Martyr's Defence," p. 284.

philosophy's intellectual war. However, intellectual pagans also employed the tools of silence or mockery. Lucian's *Peregrinus* portrayed Christians as naïve and stupid, capable of being deceived by anyone.[30] Dio Cassius (d. AD 235), even though he made express mention of the Jews[31], did not mention Christianity at all, perhaps reflecting the contempt with which it was regarded by contemporary learned paganism.[32] The Platonist Celsus in his four-volume *True Discourse* (ÆΑληθης λόγος) launched a thorough and caustic philosophical attack directed against Christianity shortly after Justin's time.[33] In Celsus' opinion, Jesus of Nazareth was a juggler, boaster and liar, the "robber chief" of a band of brigands (*Fragm.* a 2.12; 2.44b). The apostles were men of ill repute, and inventors of fictions (Origen, *Against Celsus* 2.15). The miracles ascribed to Christ, even if they were true, were no more wonderful than those performed by Egyptian magicians. Contemporary Christians were themselves liars and deceivers, stealing and falsifying ideas from the intellectual heritage of the Greeks. They were nothing more than earthworms assembled on a dunghill, vying with one another as to who was the greatest sinner (4.23). It was the height of audacity for a novel religion comprising slaves, children and ignorant women to claim possession of the truth in opposition to the collected wisdom of the ancients, a wisdom that had assisted the Roman state to world dominance (5.25 and 41). Celsus insisted that Christians ought to admit that they were not

---

30 Lucian, *Peregrinus*, 11 and 13. According to Baus, *Handbook of Church History*, p. 166, Lucian was "free from hatred against the Christians … He regarded their religious convictions and their everyday behaviour as belonging to the follies and errors which he enjoyed pillorying; but he regarded the folly of the Christians as particularly harmless."
31 Dio Cassius 37.16. 5-17.4.
32 G. T. Purves, *The Testimony of Justin Martyr to Early Christianity*, J. Nisbet, London, 1888, p. 58.
33 According to Chadwick, "Justin Martyr's Defence," p. 284, Celsus had probably read at least some of Justin's writings with care and attention.

reasonable, concede defeat in the argument, join the majority religion and give homage to the State, or face persecution to restore law and order (7.62).

(3) The Heretics

There were many during the second century AD who claimed the name of Christian, but not all believed the same doctrines Justin adhered to. In Justin's mind, this variance in beliefs constituted more than just diversity; it amounted to heresy that fragmented the unity of Christianity[34], and hindered its claim to truth. As there were philosophers who were not worthy of the name, the same was true of Christians who followed heretical teachings (*1 Apol.* 4). Justin considered heretics and their false teachings to be of the devil, and hence no heretic was a true Christian at all (*1 Apol.* 26; *Dial.* 35 and 82).

Heretics were the "enemy within" and constituted a chief danger. Nevertheless, Justin considered the existence of heretics as vindicating Christ and 'true Christians': "[the prevalence] of the spirits of error, only tends to make us adherents of the true and pure Christian doctrine more ardent in our faith and more firm in the hope he announced to us. As we look about us, we see events actually taking place which he predicted would happen in his name" (*Dial.* 35). The chief heretics who concerned Justin were the Gnostics, in particular Simon the Magician (*1 Apol.* 26, 56; *2 Apol.* 15; *Dial.* 120) and Marcion (*1 Apol.* 26, 58). Certain beliefs and practices of Jewish Christians were also of some

---

34 As Martindale, *St. Justin the Martyr*, p. 97, says, "[w]hen we read Justin's condemnation of Marcionites, Gnostics, Docetists (*1 Apol.* 26, 56, 58, etc.), we see quite clearly that he does not regard them as taking a different yet legitimate view of the same thing, but as downright outside the Church, instigated by demons, Antichrists in short."

concern.[35]

Besides their dualism and claim to a higher, non-rational knowledge of truths, the Gnostics rejected all law and morality (antinomianism) and led lives that discredited the Christian name. Firstly, there was Simon the Magician who came to Rome during the reign of the emperor Claudius with a Phoenician paramour named Helena. Announcing himself as the "great power of God" Simon made a name for himself through magical arts and was regarded by his followers (the Simonians) both in Rome and elsewhere as a god. However, Justin considered Simon to be no more than a charlatan acting under the instigation of the demons (*1 Apol.* 26). Justin was astonished that the Roman Senate could bestow honours upon Simon, while Christians went unrecognised for their virtues.[36]

Much of what we read of Simon's activities in Rome is mostly second-century legend, particularly his alleged struggles with the apostles Peter and Paul.[37] Irenaeus attributed to Simon and his followers a developed system of Gnosticism that clearly opposed the doctrines of the Roman Christians.[38] According to Irenaeus, Simon claimed at various times to be the manifestation, firstly, of the Father in Samaria, then of the

35 Justin was a major figure in the struggle against heresy (T. Stylianopoulos, *Justin Martyr and the Mosaic Law*, Society of Biblical Literature, Missoula, 1975, p. 166). As early as AD 144, he wrote denouncing the heresies prevalent among the Christians in Rome. This work, known as *Syntagma*, was most probably a response to Marcion concerning the problem of the Jewish Law. It is now entirely lost. Justin invites Antoninus Pius to read this treatise in *1 Apol.* 26. Irenaeus mentions the same work in *Against Heresies* 4.6.2.

36 Justin claimed that the Roman senate honoured Simon with a statue inscribed with the words *"Simoni Deo Sancti"* (*1 Apol.* 26). Grant, *Greek Apologists*, p. 47, states that though the Simonians boasted of this inscription as a reference to their Gnostic cult-hero and redeemer no such statue was ever erected by the Roman senate. Justin, or the Roman Christians before him, may have seen an inscription to *Semo Sancus* on the Tiber Island and mistook it as a reference to the magician.

37 See Alberto Ferreiro, *Simon Magus in Patristic, Medieval and Early Modern Traditions*, Brill, Leiden-Boston, 2005.

38 Irenaeus, *Against Heresies* 1.23; 4; 6.32.

Son in Judea, then of the Holy Spirit among the pagans. As the conception of the Deity, Helena was the mother of all, through whom the Deity created the angels and the aeons. In morality, Simon was strictly antinomian, opposing all Old Testament law. His followers during the second century continued to practise magic and led unbridled, licentious lives, in accordance with the teachings of their master. Though his importance was undoubtedly in decline by the mid-second century, Justin felt that it was still necessary to denounce Simon, as one of his contemporary apostles, Menander, retained followers who believed that through adherence to him they would never die (*1 Apol.* 26).

Marcion came to Rome from Pontus in c. AD 140 and after a few years of private study of the Scriptures began challenging the Roman presbyters on matters of interpretation and faith. Marcion's approach to the Old Testament was one of literal interpretation, rejecting allegory and subjecting it to a level of rigorous criticism that ultimately led him to discard it altogether. Marcion also rejected all the written gospels except for Luke, which he revised and edited, and stridently criticised Paul's epistles, reducing them to ten. He also produced a work of his own called *Antitheses*, which has not survived.[39]

Marcion's rejection of the Old Testament was coupled with his assertion that there was another good God greater than the Creator. Marcion's supreme God was ἀjγαθovς, good and kind; the inferior God, or Demiurge, was merely δίκαιος, righteous and just. The good God was the God of the Gospel and pure love; the inferior God was the God of the Law and tended to anger. Each God had his own sphere of operation. It was the inferior God who created the world and all its inhabitants and then elected the Jewish people as his own, making him the God of the Jews.

---

39 H. Räisänen, "Marcion," in *A Companion to Second-Century Christian "Heretics,"* Edd. A. Marjanen & P. Luomanen, Brill, Leiden, 2005, pp. 100-122 at p. 101.

Christianity was a completely new religion for Marcion, undefiled by association with Judaism.[40] Christ was not the Son of the God of the Jews, but the Son of the good God. In fact, it was the God of the Jews that had Jesus crucified and sent to Hades. There was no Old Testament prophecy relating to the coming of Christ—the Old Testament foretold only a Jewish messiah who had yet to appear. There was also no resurrection of the body "for flesh and blood shall not enter the kingdom of heaven" and no second coming of Christ in judgement, for those who rejected the good God were left to the Demiurge to cast into eternal fire.

Marcion's opposition to the flesh led to an asceticism that rejected marriage, and only virgins, widows, celibates and eunuchs could be baptised. Marcion's morality was a form of deep-seated puritanism, which he also required of his adherents. Stern morality was combined with fasting and a desire for martyrdom, both a programmatic expression of defiance against the Creator and his creation.

Marcion's doctrine of two Gods led to a formal break between himself and the Roman Church in AD 144. Having himself earlier received ordination at the hands of his father, bishop of Sinope, Marcion managed to establish an ecclesiastical organisation that both paralleled and seriously rivalled the Roman Church, flourishing extensively under the episcopate of Anicetus (AD 155-166). Those who opposed Marcion's church were considered no different than the Judaisers of the previous century.

Other heretical movements that Justin associated with the Marcionites included Valentinians, Basilidians, Saturnilians, "and others by other names; each called after the originator of the

---

40 According to Osborn, "Justin's Response," p. 38, Marcion's beliefs "endorsed the objection of the philosophers that Christianity was completely new and the objection of the Jews that Christianity was opposed to the teaching of the Old Testament."

individual opinion" (*Dial.* 35). Whether Marcion was a Gnostic has been much-debated.[41] Tertullian (*Adv. Marc.* 1.2) claimed that he had close connections with the Syrian Gnostic Cerdo, who may have influenced his views. Marcion's notion of an inferior creator God, his negative view of corporeality, and his rejection of the Old Testament approximate views commonly associated with Gnostics, but other views of his do not. For instance, Marcion recognised no divine spark in the human person, faith was emphasised more than insight or knowledge, and salvation consisted in freedom from the Creator's law rather than a return of the dispersed elements to the divinity. Perhaps the most that can be said is that Marcion's theology was rooted in Paul's thought but open to Gnostic influence.

Thirdly, there were Judaising Christians who insisted on circumcision and encouraged others to do likewise. These Jewish Christians were divided into various factions, including: (i) those who insisted that observance of the whole Mosaic Law including circumcision was necessary for salvation for both Jews and Gentile converts to Christianity; (ii) those who insisted that only circumcision, rather than observance of the whole Mosaic Law, was necessary for salvation for Jews and Gentile converts to Christianity; and (iii) those who insisted that observance of the whole Mosaic Law and circumcision were necessary for salvation only for Jewish Christians. Of these three categories only (i) and (ii) were regarded as heretics by Justin. Concerning those in category (iii) Justin insisted, "that we Christians should receive them and associate with them in every way as kinsmen and brethren" (*Dial.* 47). Justin acknowledged that there were other Christians who "boldly refuse to have conversation or meals with such persons. I

41 C. Markschies, *Gnosis: An Introduction*, trans. by J. Bowden, T & T Clark, London and New York, 2003, pp. 13-27; 86-89. As Gnosticism was not a monolith, the usefulness of the term "Gnostic" has in recent years been questioned altogether. See M. A. Williams, *Rethinking "Gnosticism": An Argument for Dismantling a Dubious Category*, Princeton University Press, Princeton, 1996.

don't agree with such Christians" (*Dial.* 47).[42]

(4) The Jews

There were, perhaps, over fifty thousand Jews living in Rome at the time of Justin.[43] Their status as a *religio licita* had been partially restored during the reign of Antoninus Pius, who repealed the restrictive measures put into place around the time of the Bar Cochba revolt of AD 132-135 by his predecessor, Hadrian. These measures had included the total forbidding of circumcision, the reading of the Law, and the observance of the Sabbath.[44] Nevertheless, Antoninus still only permitted the Jews to circumcise their own sons; any person who attempted to circumcise one who was "not of the same religion" was liable to execution.[45] A tolerable *modus vivendi* between Rome and the Jews was reached, whereby in return for the right to freely practise their religion the Jews were to abandon proselytism.[46]

Jewish hostility to Christianity was strong. Christians were considered novel upstarts who usurped the ancient Scriptures given to Israel, neglected the Law given by God to Moses, and proclaimed a messiah who suffered a criminal and shameful death. Furthermore, the Christians preached an impractical

---

42 H. Conzelmann, *Gentiles, Jews, Christians: Polemics and Apologetics in the Graeco-Roman Era*, Fortress Press, Minneapolis, 1992, p. 273, states that "the status of Jewish Christianity in the heresy-orthodoxy dispute was still an open question, even in the time of Justin …"

43 Juvenal (c. AD 129) and Dio Cassius (c. AD 229) speak of the growth of Rome's Jewish community. Roman Jews worshipped publicly in at least eleven synagogues. Jewish catacombs in Rome show that they were a Greek-speaking community.

44 In all, Hadrian prohibited twenty-one Jewish practices. In addition to the three just listed, Jews were forbidden to ordain sages, operate religious courts, gather in synagogues, recite the *Shema*, wear tefillin or tzitzit, etc. Violation of any prohibition was punishable by death. See Moshe David Herr, "Persecutions and Martyrdom in Hadrian's Day," *Scripta Hierosolymitana* 23 (1972), pp. 85-125 at pp. 94-98.

45 M. Goodman, *Mission and Conversion: Proselytizing in the Religious History of the Roman Empire*, Oxford University Press, Oxford, 1994, p. 138.

46 E. Mary Smallwood, *The Jews Under Roman Rule: From Pompey to Diocletian*, E. J. Brill, Leiden, 1976, p. 472.

gospel, while refusing to separate from the world. Tension was also magnified by Christian refusal to assist the Jews in Bar Cochba's revolt.[47] Justin makes the claim that, "in the Jewish war which lately happened Bar Cochba, the leader of the revolt of the Jews, gave orders that Christians alone should be led to terrible punishments, unless they would deny Jesus the Christ and blaspheme" (*1 Apol.* 31).

In the words of Justin, the Jews "hate and, whenever you have the power, kill us … And you cease not to curse him and those who belong to him" (*Dial.* 133). Justin was aware of the Jewish prayers of eighteen petitions, which included the *birkath-ha-minim*, or thrice-daily curse against the Christians pronounced in the Jewish synagogues (*Dial.* 16, 47, 93, 95, 123, 133; cf. *1 Apol.* 31).[48] Synagogue services at the time were open to all. One purpose of such cursing was to expose Christians who may have been present in synagogues.[49]

Justin also believed that the Jews spread calumnies about the Christians, as well as attacks against the person of Jesus of Nazareth himself (for example, that he was a magician and

---

47 B. Z. Bokser, "Justin Martyr and the Jews," *The Jewish Quarterly Review* 64 (1973), pp. 204-211 at p. 205.

48 Justin's complaints are viewed as normally referring to the twelfth benediction, 'ordered' by Samuel the Small at the request of Gamaliel II at Jamnia in AD 90: W. Horbury, "The Benediction of the *Minim* and Early Jewish-Christian Controversy," *Journal of Theological Studies* n.s. 33 (1982), pp. 19-61 at pp. 19-20. It runs: "For apostates let there be no hope, and the kingdom of insolence mayest thou uproot speedily in our days; and let the noserim and the minim perish in a moment, let them be blotted out of the book of life and let them not be written with the righteous. Blessed art thou, O Lord, who humblest the insolent." Scholars are divided over the meaning of "the noserim and the minim" in the *birkath-ha-minim*, as well as Justin's own understanding of these words. L. H. Schiffman, *Who was a Jew?*, Ktav., Hoboken, New Jersey, 1985, pp. 53-61, argues that the term *noserim* referred to Gentile Christians and *minim* to Jewish Christians. Horbury (p. 27) assumes that Justin believed that the curse applied to all Christians. T. C. G. Thornton, "Christian Understandings of the *Birkath-Ha-Minim* in the Eastern Roman Empire," *Journal of Theological Studies* n.s. 38 (1987), pp. 419-431 at p. 429, argues that the cursing referred to by Justin may have been carried out informally and spasmodically, outside the Jewish liturgy and not involving the *birkath-ha-minim*.

49 Thornton, "Christian Understandings of the *Birkath-Ha-Minim*," at p. 421.

a deceiver whose body was stolen) (*Dial.* 17, 108, 120, 133). Five times in *Dialogue* he complains about Jews spreading misconceptions about Christianity (17, 32, 93, 108, 117). These "slanders" were spread by emissaries, not only to Jewish communities of the Diaspora, but to "every land" (*Dial.* 17). Justin himself entered into debate with a number of Jewish evangelists (*Dial.* 50). Justin considered Jewish teachers in general "blind," "unintelligent," "foolish," and "selfish" (*Dial.* 68), and responsible for misleading their people with false interpretations of Scripture.[50]

Scholarly opinion originally advocated the prevalence of intense missionary rivalry between Jews and Christians within second-century Rome. According to Nilson[51], proselytism was practised by both, with curious Gentiles unaware of the differences between Christianity and Judaism the most competed-for converts. In fact, Jewish efforts among Gentiles were said to be extensive enough to hamper Christian evangelisation. It was also believed that the edicts of Hadrian and Antoninus against circumcision of non-Jews evidenced a pre-existing and successful proselytising effort among Gentiles. There may also have occurred debates with Christians before Gentile audiences, supported by prominent Jewish leaders and teachers visiting Rome.[52] These debates took place even

---

50 T. J. Horner, "Justin's Mission to the Jews," *The Covenant Quarterly* 56/4 (1998), pp. 33-44 at p. 40, says, "It is difficult to know who these teachers were. The mid-second century C.E. is too early to assume any significant rabbinic influence outside Palestine."

51 J. Nilson, "To whom is Justin's *Dialogue with Trypho* addressed?," *Journal of Theological Studies*, n.s. 38 (1977), pp. 538-546 at p. 539.

52 G. La Piana, "Foreign Groups in Rome during the First Centuries of the Empire," *Harvard Theological Review* 20 (1927), pp. 183-403 at p. 371. A. B. Hulen, "The 'Dialogues with the Jews' as sources for the early Jewish argument against Christianity," *Journal of Biblical Literature* 51 (1932), pp. 58-70 at p. 59, states, "It is certain that there was no lack of personal debates regarding the relative merits of the two religions … The Talmud makes mention of them "

though Justin mentions that Jews were forbidden to speak with Christians (*Dial.* 38, 112).

This picture of missionary rivalry, however, has been seriously challenged in more recent decades. Cohen[53] believes that Judaism was probably never missionary and certainly abandoned all proselytising after Hadrian. Goodman[54] examines second-century rabbinic texts, laws passed by the Roman state, Greek and Latin inscriptions made by Jews and even religious works composed by Christians, concluding that Jews continued to accept Gentiles who offered themselves up to be converts but, with some individual exceptions, generally never adopted the enthusiastic proselytism found among Christians. The strength of this conclusion mainly rests on the lack of rabbinic literature on conversion that alludes to proselytism and the nature of the rabbinic conversion ceremony, which possessed an air of *fait accompli* and had faithful Jews present more or less only as witnesses of the convert's intent. As for the imperial ban on circumcision, this may have reflected more a horror of mutilation as well as Rome's own desire to restrict Judaism rather than any actual Jewish enthusiasm for converts.[55]

(5) The General Public (Popular Calumnies)

Justin refers to popular calumnies towards the end of *2 Apology* when speaking of the "wicked disguise" thrown around the doctrines of the Christians to deter others from joining them (*2 Apol.* 13). This "disguise" had many facets, was widely circulated, and had its roots in the words and writings of learned and unlearned Romans alike.

---

53 J. S. Cohen, *Conversion to Judaism: A History and Analysis*, Ktav, Hoboken, NJ, 1992, p. 39.
54 Goodman, *Mission and Conversion*, pp. 130 and 132. By the third century there was little change. According to Goodman, "some Jews had begun to see proselytizing as a religious duty, but there was no unanimity on the subject, and much ambivalence even within the restricted society of the rabbis" (at p. 148).
55 Goodman, *Mission and Conversion*, pp. 138-139.

While investigating Christians in Bithynia in AD 112, Pliny the Younger reported to Trajan that they bound themselves with an oath not to perform "any crime" and that they met "for a meal which was ordinary and harmless."[56] Other second-century Romans, however, wrote very differently of the Christians, accusing them, *inter alia*, of atheism, political disloyalty,[57] sexual debauchery, ritual murder and cannibalism. Justin was fully aware of these accusations (*1 Apol.* 6-12). One such writer was Lollianus, whose work of fiction alleged that Christians during their worship roasted the hearts of children and distributed portions to initiates, "and when they were holding them (swore) an oath by the blood of the heart"[58] Marcus Cornelius Fronto recounted stories of Christians worshipping the head of an ass, accompanied with luxurious meals, rites of drunkenness, incestuous orgies and the drinking of infant blood.[59] Celsus wrote accusing Christian presbyters of practising magic and using books that contained the names of demons.[60]

Whether false or not, charges of such seriousness increased

---

56 Pliny, *Epistle* 10.96.

57 Popular mistrust of Christianity would certainly have been reinforced if the Romans read for themselves the very writings of the Christians: Justin described the Roman Gods as "… evil and ungodly demons" (*1 Apol.* 5); his disciple, Tatian the Syrian, *Address to the Greeks* 28 and 35, c. AD 170, wrote, "I reject your legislation also, for there ought to be one common polity for all"; Irenaeus, *Against Heresies* 4.30.3, c. AD 180, spoke of the "Romans and other nations" as peoples separate from the Christians; while Tertullian, *Apology* 39, boldly asserted that "Nothing is more foreign to us than the State."

58 Lollianus, papyrus fragment first or second century AD. Taken from M. Aquilina, *The Mass of the Early Christians*, Our Sunday Visitor Publishing, Huntington, Indiana, 2001, pp. 128-129.

59 In Minucius Felix, *Octavius* 9. Fronto (d. AD 166) was consul in AD 143 and a former tutor of Marcus Aurelius. It is noteworthy that both pagans and Christians knew his attack, which formed part of a speech delivered c. AD 157, and its effect lasted well into the third century when Minucius wrote his *Octavius*.

60 In Origen, *Against Celsus*, 6.40-41.

the danger for all early Christians.[61] The pagan popular response was often "Out with the Christians!"[62], or "Away with the atheists!"[63] Lurid tales of immorality incited mob action,[64] made Christians scapegoats for the disasters that afflicted the empire,[65] triggered waves of new arrests and imprisonment, or convinced governors to launch or intensify persecution.[66]

61 According to J. Daniélou, *The Christian Centuries: The First Six Hundred Years*, Darton, Longman and Todd, London, 1964, p. 88, "We may note that Justin suggests that the charges brought against the Christians were perhaps true of the Gnostics. It is certain that in pagan eyes Christians of the Great Church, Montanists and Gnostics of various kinds were confused. The same thing will be found in Celsus, and this muddle was doubtless very damaging to the Christians."
62 Lucian, *Alexander*, 38.
63 Eusebius, *History of the Church*, 6.15.18-19.
64 Tertullian, *Apology* 37: "How often, too, the hostile mob, paying no regard to you, takes the law into its own hand, and assails us with stones and flames! With the very frenzy of the Bacchanals, they do not even spare the Christian dead, but tear them, now sadly changed, no longer entire, from the rest of the tomb, from the asylum we might say of death, cutting them in pieces, rending them asunder."
65 Tertullian, *Apology* 40: "If the Tiber rises as high as the city walls, if the Nile does not send its waters up over the fields, if the heavens give no rain, if there is an earthquake, if there is famine or pestilence, straightway the cry is, 'Away with the Christians to the lion!'"
66 M. Grant, *Augustine to Constantine: The Thrust of the Christian Movement into the Roman World*, Collins Publisher, London, 1971, p. 114, comments: "[During the martyrdom of Christians at Lyons in 177] household slaves under interrogation claimed that their Christian masters were given to [cannibalism and incest]. In consequence, even the more moderate-minded citizens of Lyons became hostile towards their Christian neighbours."

Chapter 3

Christian Apology and the Rhetorical and Literary Conventions of the Second-Century Graeco-Roman World

What is apologetic literature?

According to Grant, "apologetic literature emerges from minority groups that are trying to come to terms with the larger culture within which they live. [To achieve this, the apologist tries] to interpret his own culture—religious, philosophical, or artistic, as the case may be—to the broader group."[67] Rokéah, who refers to these same words of Grant, puts it in the following terms: "the distinguishing feature of the apologists is their … attempt to arrive at a *modus vivendi* with the general culture within which they live, by searching for points of contact between them."[68]

Concerning the Christian apologists of the second century,

---

67 Grant, *Greek Apologists*, p. 9.
68 D. Rokéah, *Justin Martyr and the Jews*, Brill, Leiden, 2002, p. ix.

Grant[69] notes, "some ... simply try to vindicate their own culture and religion ... and usually try to prove that theirs is more ancient, more authentic, and more expressive of common values." Young[70] sums up their efforts in terms of justification: "justification of their unpopular—indeed, potentially dangerous—decision to turn their backs on the classical literature inherited from antiquity and the customs of their forefathers" However, the overall aim of the Christian apologists was more broad and ambitious. As Barnard states:

> ... *apologia*, or the case for the defence, embraced far more than the refutation of ... attacks—and that was not difficult. It was based on the magnificent defence that Socrates had made at his trial before the people of Athens in which he demonstrated the essential rationality of his position. The Christian Apologists therefore set themselves the wider task of showing how Christianity was the embodiment of the noblest conceptions of Greek philosophy and was the truth *par excellence*. Their object was not only to appeal for toleration but even more to win their readers to the Christian faith. In addition they were concerned with the questionings of thoughtful people.[71]

Apology's relationship to petitions to the Roman emperors
The writings of the apologists were mostly in the form of legal documents, petitions requesting the state to carefully investigate the real nature of Christianity.[72] In presenting their

---

69 Grant, *Greek Apologists*, p. 9.
70 F. Young, "Greek Apologists of the Second Century," in *Apologetics in the Roman Empire: Pagans, Jews and Christians*, edd. M. Edwards, M. Goodman & S. Price, Oxford University Press, Oxford, 1999, p. 81.
71 Barnard, *St. Justin Martyr*, p. 2.
72 Grant, "The Chronology of the Greek Apologists," p. 30.

communications the apologists needed to respect and follow the proper classical literary and rhetorical conventions of the day, as was the general concern of ancient writers.[73] This need was heightened by the fact that most of the apologists addressed the emperors personally. Imperial hearings included both embassies as well as legal cases.[74] Despite their workload, the emperors were known to occasionally allot generous amounts of time to hear the speeches of ambassadors sent to them to obtain relief for those whom the ambassador represented. They also usually devoted countless hours deciding court cases, both making the decision and announcing the same.[75] In cases marginal to the affairs of the empire the emperor often cut the whole procedure short and decided the matter based upon answers to given questions.

Justin's two *Apologies* both possess the form of those speeches delivered to emperors seeking the granting of requests. In *1 Apology* 68 Justin yearns for judgement to be given "as we have asked" and that "what we ask is just." This is the language of petition, a language that appears also in *2 Apology* when Justin refers to his work as a βιβλίδιον, or *libellus* (petition). Some have little doubt that length-wise *2 Apology* was appropriate if Justin intended to deliver it as a speech before the emperor.[76] However, given the length of *1 Apology* it is more likely that

---

73 A. J. Guerra, "The Conversion of Marcus Aurelius and Justin Martyr: The Purpose, Genre, and Content of the First Apology," *The Second Century* 9 (1992), pp. 129-187 at pp. 174-175.

74 Guerra, "The Conversion of Marcus Aurelius," n. 15, p. 174. The embassy, involving an ambassador's speech, became the most important means by which a group, city, region or state presented their interests before the emperor. The ambassador's speech came into its own as a distinct genre of deliberative oratory during the Hellenistic period: see C. W. Wooten, "The Ambassador's Speech: A Particular Hellenistic Genre of Oratory," *Quarterly Journal of Speech* 59 (1973), pp. 209-212 at p. 209.

75 W. Schoedel, "Apologetic Literature and Ambassadorial Activities," *Harvard Theological Review* 82 (1989), pp. 55-78 at p. 57.

76 Schoedel, "Apologetic Literature," p. 59.

Justin intended to present this work to the emperor for his reading rather than to deliver it before him orally. Yet, a problem arises if any of these works were intended as written petitions. According to Buck[77], a *libellus* written and addressed to Roman emperors was usually only a few pages in length, much shorter than any of the works of Justin. That being so, perhaps Justin never intended to deliver his apologies before the emperors and thus felt unimpeded by considerations of prolixity.

Another possibility is that Justin employed a new form of apology invented by Christian apologists that was a mixture of explanation and petition. This mixture is evident in *1 Apology* where amidst the language of petition appears words such as "address" (προσφώνησις) and "explanation" (ἐξήγησις), evidencing Justin's intention to include important information about Christian belief, behaviour and worship. Thus, we have emerging apology enclosed in petition and subservient to the purpose of petition. Schoedel calls this "apologetically grounded petition," a significant literary vehicle with no previous precedent in the Graeco-Roman literary tradition.[78]

Rhetorical features typically found in petitions

Since petitions presented to the emperors sought to persuade them to do something it is necessary to look at the standard methods by which persuasion was achieved in ancient literature, viz., rhetoric, and the extent to which Christian apologies conformed to these standards.

Rhetoric is the art of language as an instrument of persuasion.[79] Aristotle defined rhetoric "as the faculty of

---

77 P. Lorraine Buck, "Athenagoras's *Embassy*: A Literary Fiction," *Harvard Theological Review* 89 (1996) pp. 209-226 at p. 210.

78 Schoedel, "Apologetic Literature," p. 78.

79 J. G. Cook, "The Protreptic Power of Early Christian Language from John to Augustine," *Vigiliae Christianae* 48 (1994), pp. 105-134 at p. 105.

discovering the possible means of persuasion in reference to any subject whatever."[80] Its importance to the educated and literate Greek or Roman and its influence on ancient literature cannot be over-emphasised.[81] Developed originally by the Greeks, rhetoric was adapted later by the Romans for their own oratory and writings. The most famous Roman rhetoricians were Cicero, Seneca the Elder, Tacitus, Pliny the Younger, Quintilian, and Fronto.

According to Dunn[82], "much of classical rhetoric was standard and uniform across the schools of thought and particular authors." Petitions of all kinds in the ancient world employed rhetoric. Rhetoric is divided into three kinds corresponding to three audiences: deliberative; forensic; epideictic.

Deliberative (or protreptic) rhetoric involves the use of exhortation and dissuasion about matters pertaining to the future. It is oriented towards policy and thus the hearer considers the future and whether to adopt or change a certain course of action or whether proposed laws would be expedient or harmful.

Forensic rhetoric uses accusation or defence about matters pertaining to the past. Forensic speeches typically embellish the facts, usually with great vivacity, to persuade the hearer of the guilt or innocence of a person or persons in regard to a past action. Forensic rhetoric is the rhetoric of the law court.

Epideictic rhetoric employs praise or blame about present matters. Like forensic speeches, epideictic addresses are embellished statements of fact, also given with great vivacity, to persuade the hearer of the praiseworthiness of blameworthiness of an individual, group or idea. It is typically concerned with

---

80 Aristotle, *The Art of Rhetoric*, 1.2.15 (1355b).
81 G. D. Dunn, *Tertullian*, Routledge, London and New York, 2004, p. 25.
82 G. D. Dunn, "The Universal Spread of Christianity as a Rhetorical Argument in Tertullian's *Adversus Judaeos*," *Journal of Early Christian Studies* 8:1 (2000), pp. 1-19 at p. 3.

the hearer's present belief.

Linked with rhetoric, the ancient rhetor used various kinds of proofs (πίστεων) to persuade an audience: ethos (εθος), logos (λόγος), and pathos (πάθος). The ethos was the moral character of the speaker, the logos was the speaker's address containing the rational arguments, and pathos was the rousing of the hearers to a certain emotion with the intention of leading them to a desired decision. In addition to the proofs there were five functions a rhetor needed to master for success: invention of arguments; proper sequencing of arguments; style, or choice of words; memorisation; and delivery (voice and bodily gesture).

Wooten[83] outlines the rhetorical features that typically appeared in ancient ambassadorial petitions presented before rulers:

(1) A mood-setting introduction (*exordium*).
(2) A forensic review of the history of relations between the two parties that constituted the narration (*narratio*). This may have included the emphasising of past favours bestowed upon the addressee.
(3) Praise of or even an attack (sometimes slanderous) upon the addressee (epideictic rhetoric).
(4) The ambassador's proposal couched in arguments of honour, self-interest or both. It was an argument of honour if the proposal was said to be consistent and just in relation to historical precedent, oaths or treaties. It was an argument of self-interest if the proposal was said to advantage the addressee (deliberative rhetoric). An ambassador employing self-interest would seek to point out consequences, arousing either fear or love (*pathos*).
(5) The *peroration*, wherein the ambassador returned

---

83 Wooten, "The Ambassador's Speech," pp. 210-211.

to the arguments to urge the addressee to act in accordance with their finest traditions (deliberative rhetoric).

It was not necessary that all three elements of deliberative, forensic and epideictic rhetoric be present in the one petition, though such was possible. Usually the deliberative stood to the fore.

Like non-Christian rhetoricians, ancient Christians endeavoured to employ the language of persuasion. The authors of scripture certainly showed some degree of familiarity with classical rhetoric.[84] In the post-apostolic writers, the adoption of classical rhetoric was closely connected with the partial adoption of classical philosophy originating in Platonism, Aristotelianism and Stoicism.[85] Some Christians thought this to be idle or even a pride in worldly achievements but ultimately the view prevailed that eloquence had a place in explaining the faith to outsiders and deepening the practice of it among Christians. Eventually, there even developed, especially in Latin, a vigour in early Christian writing lacking in contemporary pagan counterparts, due largely to the intensity of Christian opinion against paganism.[86]

Schoedel[87] illustrates with reference to Athenagoras and Justin that Christian apologies usually opened with standard strategies to render the judge well disposed to the apologist's cause. There followed an *exordium* outlining the reason why the work was written. The *narratio* outlined the history of the

---

84 See A. N. Wilder, *Early Christian Rhetoric: The Language of the Gospel*, Hendrickson, Peabody, Massachusetts, 1964; G. A. Kennedy, *New Testament Interpretation Through Rhetorical Criticism*, University of North Carolina Press, Chapel Hill, 1984; B. L. Mack, *Rhetoric and the New Testament*, Guides to Biblical Scholarship, Fortress Press, Minneapolis, 1990.
85 G. A. Kennedy, *Greek Rhetoric Under Christian Emperors*, Princeton University Press, Princeton, New Jersey, 1983, p. 183.
86 G. A. Kennedy, *Classical Rhetoric and its Christian and Secular Tradition from Ancient to Modern Times*, The University of North Carolina Press, Chapel Hill, 1980, p. 134.
87 Schoedel, "Apologetic Literature," pp. 55-56.

relationship between Judeo-Christianity and Graeco-Roman civilisation while the *partitio* set out the points at issue and the author's position. The length of certain apologies resulting from the refutation of "charges" (for example, atheism, Thyestean feasts, Oedipean intercourse) indicates forensic models employing either confirmation (*confirmatio*) or refutation (*refutatio*). An *apodeixis* or "demonstration" would provide an outline of prophecy and the life of Christ. Dialectic was adopted in an attempt to explain and defend Christian beliefs. Attempting to convince and persuade people to live in accord with Christian teachings falls within the realm of deliberative rhetoric. Kennedy[88] observes that the apologists explained scripture using the arts of definition, division and syllogistic reasoning and utilised Attic language and style. All this was done to enable Christianity to be understood and taken seriously by the educated pagan.[89]

Nevertheless, Christianity still possessed a distinctive rhetoric originating in Jewish attitudes found in the Old Testament and reflecting the new theology of Jesus and his apostles. Kennedy[90] sums it up as follows:

> Christian rhetoric presupposes the intervention of God in history and through the Holy Spirit in the minds of men. For the classical ethos of the speaker it substitutes divine authority given canonisation in the Scriptures and the revelation accorded to the Church; for probable argument as a basis of proof it substitutes proclamation of the kerygma, or divine message, but preserves the forms of inductive and deductive argument; for supporting evidence it

---

88 Kennedy, *Greek Rhetoric*, p. 184.
89 W. Kinsig, "Der Sitz im Leben der Apologie in der Alten Kirche," *Zeitschrift für Kirchengeschichte* 100 (1989): pp. 291-317 at p. 291.
90 *Greek Rhetoric*, pp. 180-181.

turns to miracles and the acts of the martyrs; and for pathos the Christian author threatens damnation or promises eternal life. Christian rhetoric has distinctive topics and a distinctive style based largely on the language of the psalmists and the prophets … It is also characteristic of Christian rhetoric that whatever the text or the occasion, all details are made subordinate to one message, "Jesus Christ and him crucified."

Justin's use of rhetorical strategies

Justin himself possessed a familiarity with philosophical argument and other forms of literature and though he criticised rhetoric he certainly employed it.[91] Keresztes[92] notes that in Justin's writings there is the "use of an excessive rhetorical art." Depending on one's perspective, Justin was either a mediocre rhetorician who was only partially familiar with classical rhetorical methods or was a Christian radical who was willing to be independent and try something beyond Christian convention.

As mentioned above, Justin described *1 Apology* as an "address" (προσφώνησις), which the rhetorician Menander defined as "a speech of praise to rulers spoken by an individual."[93] Such addresses typically emphasised the humane qualities of the addressee, particular justice, gentleness, affability, integrity, impartiality and incorruptibility. Before outlining his deliberative objectives Justin touches upon these very themes in the first seven chapters of *1 Apology* when contrasting the unfair

---

91 During his formative years Justin was brought up in Gentile customs and was provided with a Greek education (*Dial.* 2). Though not a master of contemporary thought and culture, Justin had read a sufficient amount of Greek poetry, philosophy and history to pronounce on their value.
92 "Literary Genre," at p. 100.
93 Grant, *Greek Apologists*, p. 54.

treatment of Christians with what it should be.

There is some debate among commentators as to the literary model for Justin's *Apologies*. Barnard[94] proposes that "it seems unlikely that Justin based his work [*1 Apology*] on the Classical oration or on any other ancient literary artifice ... his Apology is his own and cannot be fitted into any pre-determined plan—hence the digressions and repetitions." Against Barnard, Wehofer[95] suggests that Justin's literary and rhetorical model for *1 Apology* was the *Apology* of Plato due to a substantial thematic parallel; namely, both writers were concerned about speaking the truth.[96] Contrary to this, Guerra[97] argues that Aristotle's *Protrepticus* affords the positive parallel. There is also the *Protreptic* of Isocrates, a contemporary of Aristotle. Both of these pagan writers wrote to kings seeking to demonstrate that philosophy was essential for practical living with the latter adding that conversion to the philosophical way of life would also ensure arrival to the "Isles of the Blest." Similarly, Justin's protreptic presents Christianity to the emperors as a divine philosophy that is not only essential for right living but also to attain eternal life (*1 Apol.* 17, 19). Failure on the part of the emperors to convert to the true philosophy will leave them without excuse before God (*1 Apol.* 3, 68). Other motifs shared by Aristotle and Justin include contempt of death (*1 Apol.* 11), polemic against Academics and Epicureans, and the metaphors of doing battle and athletic exercise to acquire virtue (*1 Apol.* 14).

Keresztes[98] identifies four main groups of arguments in *1 Apology* emerging after a brief *partitio* in *1 Apol.* 3 for the purposes of determining Justin's rhetorical devices: a

---

94 *Justin Martyr*, p. 17.

95 Th. Wehofer, *Die Apologie Justins des Philosopher und Märtyrers in literarhistorischer Beziehung zum erstenmal untersucht* (Römische Quartalschrift, Suppl. 6, 1897), p. 85.

96 Plato, *Apology* 18a; Justin, *1 Apol.* 2.

97 "The Conversion of Marcus Aurelius," p. 177.

98 "The Literary Genre," p. 101.

refutation of certain charges against Christians (*1 Apol.* 5-12); a loose collection of certain Christian teachings (*1 Apol.* 14-22); an illustration of the uniqueness of Christ and the superiority of his teachings (*1 Apol.* 23-60); and a description of Christian rituals (*1 Apol.* 61-67). Keresztes recognises each group of arguments as either a rhetorical or philosophical thesis or hypothesis connected by perorations, transitions, exordia, etc.

The word *enteuxis* means a plea or petition and well describes Justin's *Second Apology*. The literary style of *2 Apology* conforms precisely to that of a speech delivered before an audience. It even calls itself a speech (λόγοι σύνταξιν) in its opening paragraph (*2 Apol.* 1). According to Erhardt[99], *2 Apology* "is a strongly emotional, passionate harangue" delivered in protest of the outrage perpetrated by the notoriously brutal *praefectus urbis* Q. Lollius Urbicus. In fact, it is filled throughout with a strong rhetorical *pathos*.

As previously mentioned, rhetoricians frequently sought to arouse emotions such as fear, anger and pity to alter an audience's judgement. Christian writers aroused fear through the threat of eternal punishment. Justin does this in *2 Apology* in his account of the Christian woman who sought to persuade her husband to live a sober life. She threatened him with hell-fire as the penalty for failing to change his lifestyle. However, he failed to respond to her deliberative rhetoric and instead denounced her to the authorities as a Christian (*2 Apol.* 2). Justin also refers to eternal punishment in a defence of it as Christian teaching in *2 Apol.* 9.

The climactic chapter of *2 Apology* is chapter 12 with a final deliberative exhortation to "Change: think again." In the lead-up, Justin employed the following techniques: as part of *logos* in support of his demand for judicial justice Justin highlighted the

---

99 A. Ehrhardt, "Justin Martyr's Two Apologies," *Journal of Ecclesiastical History* 4 (1953), pp. 1-12 at p. 7.

inconsistency of supposedly wicked men and women willingly dying heroic deaths when they could easily have avoided such by false denials; as part of *pathos* Justin attempted to evoke emotion by recounting the unjust way Christian domestics, frail women and children were denounced and tortured into making false admissions; as part of *ethos* Justin announced the Christian God as the observer and the ultimate judge of all; and in denouncing those who accused Christians of evils they themselves committed Justin employed the epideictic rhetoric of blame.

Though not an Apology in petition form, the *Dialogue* "is an essential development within Justin's apologetical enterprise."[100] The form is that of a Platonic dialogue, exhibiting the hallmark characteristics of such a model: a relaxed opening, questions, objections, cross-examination, shifts of ground, expostulations, admissions of defeat, and reducing the adversary to silence.[101] The ability to engage in such discourse was the primary mark of education in Justin's time.

Since Plato's time, dialogues were employed in various ways for the purpose at arriving at eternal truths.[102] In Justin's case he fitted a Platonic literary form to defend Christianity and refute pagan philosophy and Judaism. Beginning in the opening chapters (*Dial.* 1-8) there is the chance encounter with an old man setting the stage for a serious discussion *à la* Socrates. The Socratic question-and-answer method and stress on definition

---

100 Young, "Greek Apologists of the Second Century," p. 84.

101 T. Rajak, "Talking at Trypho: Christian Apologetic as Anti-Judaism in Justin's *Dialogue with Trypho the Jew*," in *Apologetics in the Roman Empire: Pagans, Jews and Christians*, edd. M. Edwards, M. Goodman & S. Price, Oxford University Press, pp. 59-80 at p. 63.

102 S. Denning-Bolle, "Christian Dialogue as Apologetic: The Case of Justin Martyr seen in Historical Context," *Bulletin of the John Rylands Library* 69 (1986-87), pp. 492-510 at p. 492. In fact, Plato's contribution to defining the discipline of dialectic ("controversial method") stretched well into the Middle Ages: Denning-Bolle, "Christian Dialogue as Apologetic," p. 493.

is used to expose Justin's inadequate knowledge about the soul's immortality, its ability to see God and the superiority of the prophets. Ironically, Platonic dialectic becomes Justin's tool to exhibit Christianity's superior claim to truth and unity over Platonism itself.

Justin's stylised conversion account illustrates the functioning of rhetorical *pathos*. "Love" is one word Justin used to characterise how he was persuaded: "Love of the prophets and of those men who are friends of Christ came over me" (*Dial.* 8).

There are four major groups of arguments employed by Justin in *Dialogue:* Christian superiority, fulfilled prophecy, miracles and True Israel. The claim of Christianity's superiority over the philosophies of paganism sought to achieve the deliberative-protreptic aim of moving unattached Gentiles to consider Christianity as the "only safe and useful philosophy." Justin also outlined this argument to fortify Christians against Judaism, Judaising Christians and Marcionism. The references to Christ's miracles (*Dial.* 69, et al) were similarly intended to serve deliberative and educational purposes, namely, to convert unattached Gentiles and fortify Christians in their encounters with Jews. The vast section on fulfilled prophecy (*Dial.* 31-108) is an *apodeixis* demonstrating the claims of Jesus of Nazareth as the expected messiah.

Justin's collection of arguments asserting the Christians as the True Israel (*Dial.* 109-141) constitutes another *apodeixis*. Both 'proof from prophecy' and 'True Israel' were likewise intended to serve either protreptic or educational purposes.

Chapter 4

The Destination and Purpose of Justin's Apologetical Works

To whom did Justin write? Were Justin's works all intended for the same audience? Did Justin intend his works to have singular or multiple destinations? Why did Justin write and what did he hope to gain?

In this chapter these questions will be considered with respect to both Justin's *Apologies* and *Dialogue*. Once destination is determined, the structure of Justin's works will be analysed to ascertain his apologetical purposes. In determining both destination and purpose current scholarly opinion will be outlined and critiqued.

Once determined, Justin's apologetical purposes will be ranked in order of importance. Was Justin only concerned with establishing a *modus vivendi* between Christians and the world around them, or did he also seek other goals, such as the vindication of Christianity over paganism and Judaism and the conversion of his audience? Did he possess any other motivation?

Destination and purpose of the Apologies

Scholars generally agree that Justin wrote his *Apologies* in Rome in the middle of the second century, sometime between AD 148 and 161.[1] If we accept the opinion of Grant[2], Justin wrote *1 Apology* no earlier than AD 155, with *2 Apology* following very soon afterwards.

Much scholarly ink has also been expended on the relationship between *1 Apology* and *2 Apology*. Goodenough[3] regards *2 Apology* as separate from *1 Apology*, and only a fragment of a much larger original work. Keresztes[4] argues that *2 Apology* is a work of rhetoric unconnected with *1 Apology*. Grant[5] holds that *1 Apology* and *2 Apology* are really one work, with *1 Apology* being occasioned by the martyrdom of St Polycarp of Smyrna and *2 Apology* being a second part inspired by then-recent events in Rome. Osborn[6] says similarly that *2 Apology* "has all the marks of an urgent addition." Barnard[7] and Stylianopoulos[8] believe that *2 Apology* was designed as a supplement to *1 Apology* and may have been appended to second editions of *1 Apology*. There is no agreed position about this question, which is complicated by the words of Eusebius[9] who, it can be deduced, knew *1 Apology* and *2 Apology* as *1 Apology*, and referred to a separate work, now probably lost, as *2 Apology*.

---

1 W. A. Jurgens, *The Faith of the Early Fathers*, vol. 1, The Liturgical Press, Collegeville, Minnesota, 1970, pp. 50, 57, 58; Quasten, *Patrology*, vol. 1, p. 199.

2 Grant, *Greek Apologists*, pp. 53-54.

3 E. R. Goodenough, *The Theology of Justin Martyr*, Philo Press, Amsterdam, 1968, pp. 84-88.

4 P. Keresztes, "The So-called Second Apology of Justin," p. 867.

5 R. M. Grant, "The Fragments of the Greek Apologists and Irenaeus," in *Biblical and Patristic Studies in Memory of R. P. Casey*, J. N. Birdsall ed., Herder, Freiburg, 1963, pp. 54-55.

6 Osborn, *Justin Martyr*, p. 11.

7 Barnard, *St. Justin Martyr*, p. 10.

8 Stylianopoulos, "Justin Martyr," p. 648.

9 Eusebius, *History of the Church*, 4.16-17.

Traditionally, the vast majority of scholars accepted without question that Justin's *Apologies* were intended either to be directly read to or delivered into the hands of the Roman emperors and/or the Senate.[10] This is due to the internal evidence of the opening addresses[11] and Justin's own description of his works as an "address" and "petition" (*1 Apol.* 1; *2 Apol.* 14) and explanation (*1 Apol.* 68). There is also the external testimony of Eusebius in his *History of the Church*, who states:

> Justin, in addition to his admirable work *Against the Greeks*, addressed other compositions containing *A Defence of our Faith* to the Emperor Antoninus, surnamed Pius, and to the Roman Senate.[12]
>
> At the same period, Justin, whom I mentioned a little way back, after presenting a second book in defence of our doctrines to the rulers already named, was honoured by a divine martyrdom.[13]

Barnard states that the mode of address of *1 Apology* is similar to that of Hellenistic Jewish writers who sought a sympathetic hearing for their requests, and that "it is not to be supposed that Justin's *Apologies* never reached the emperors,"[14] especially as the Antonines received and heard an enormous number of

---

10 For example, Ehrhardt, "Justin Martyr's Two Apologies," p. 5; Keresztes, "Literary Genre," p. 109; R. M. Grant, "Forms and Occasions of the Greek Apologists," *Studi e materiali di storia delle religioni* 52 (1986), p. 216.

11 Justin, *1 Apol.* 1: "To the Emperor Titus Aelius Adrianus Antoninus Pius Augustus Caesar; to his son Verissimus the Philosopher; to Lucius the Philosopher, by birth son of Caesar and by adoption son of Pius, an admirer of learning; to the sacred Senate and to the whole Roman people"; Justin, *2 Apol.* 1: "To the Roman Senate. The things that have lately taken place in your city under Urbicus ... have forced me to compose this address for you Romans who are men of feeling like ours and are our brethren."

12 Eusebius, *History of the Church*, 4.11.11.

13 Eusebius, *History of the Church*, 4.16.1.

14 Barnard, *St. Justin Martyr: The First and Second Apologies*, p. 6.

petitions from private individuals as well as public officials.[15] Ehrhardt[16] states that both *Apologies* contain applications to one or other of the imperial offices, and convincingly argues from *2 Apol.* 14 that *2 Apology* was a petition (βιβλίδιον) normally handed in to the imperial chancery by a private individual.

Further evidence suggesting an intention on Justin's part to deliver his *Apologies* to the emperors is the inclusion of Marcus' name amongst the list of addressees. Why did Justin not simply address his petitions to the reigning emperor Antoninus Pius? This was probably because, as Guerra states, Antoninus Pius had by this time publicly announced his decision to share his rule with Marcus, and from AD 147 Marcus acted as "virtual co-emperor," giving advice readily heeded by Pius. Hence, Justin was careful to frame his addresses as it would have been "highly impolitic" to omit the name of Marcus. Such precision would not necessarily be expected if the *Apologies* were intended only for internal use among Christians.

Even though there is evidence that Justin intended his *Apologies* for the emperors he may certainly have had another simultaneous audience in mind. He knew that *libelli* and the imperial responses to them were attached together and openly displayed near to the emperor's residence. After one month the petitions were taken down and archived. In Rome, petitions were displayed in the "Porticus of the Trajan Springs." This site was chosen due to its ideal setting. There were baths and social gatherings, a marketplace, cooks, jugglers, prostitutes, and placards on display. Justin had reason to hope that his petition and the response thereto would eventually be displayed in this open forum, reaching and hopefully influencing a maximum number of the general public.

---

15 See F. Millar, *The Emperor in the Roman World: 31 B.C.- A.D. 337*, Duckworth, London, 1977, pp. 507-516.
16 Ehrhardt, "Justin Martyr's two Apologies," pp. 4-5 & 7.

However, two significant problems arise if it is to be argued that Justin intended the emperors to receive and read his *Apologies*. The first relates to their size. Those intending to address an emperor either verbally or in writing were required to do so within the framework of the legal or quasi-legal hearings the emperor granted individuals in important cases. Though emperors were known at times to be generous (allowing hours rather than minutes) there were time-limits measured by a water-clock, or *clepsydra*. Being sixty-eight chapters in length, *1 Apology* presents the largest and most obvious difficulty and there is still debate as regards *2 Apology*. Schoedel[17] considers the latter's size appropriate for a petition before the emperor; however, Millar[18] argues that it too "is substantially longer than any *libelli* known to us from inscriptions or papyri." Excessive length, coupled with the pariah status already officially heaped upon the Christians,[19] would have made Justin's *Apologies* highly vulnerable to ruthless rejection by officious Roman administrators and exposed Justin to serious repercussions. Thus, it is extremely unlikely that they ever reached the attention of the emperors even if that were Justin's intention.[20]

The second problem relates to the form of the *Apologies*. Contrary to Guerra, Buck[21] observes that *1 Apology*,

> while seemingly formal and official, contains three

---

17 Schoedel, "Apologetic Literature," p. 59.

18 Millar, *The Emperor*, p. 563.

19 Christianity's pariah status alone could have prevented any petition from Justin ever reaching the emperors. According to Buck, "Athenagoras's *Embassy*," p. 217, "Christians were accorded neither rights nor privileges … It is hardly likely … that a Christian would have been granted a hearing before the emperor to defend his faith when that faith was a criminal offense." See also Robin Lane Fox, *Pagans and Christians*, Knopf, New York, 1987, pp. 305-306.

20 This is the view also of A. Birley, *Marcus Aurelius: A Biography* (rev. ed.), New Haven, Yale, 1987, p. 112 and P. Lorraine Buck, "Justin Martyr's *Apologies*: Their Number, Destination, and Form," *Journal of Theological Studies*, n.s. 54 (2003), pp. 45-59 at p. 51.

21 Buck, "Justin Martyr's *Apologies*," p. 51.

careless and inexcusable errors. First … the correct and complete title for the Emperor Antoninus Pius places the title Caesar, not following Augustus as Justin has it, but directly following Emperor … moreover, documents from Egypt dating from the reign of Antoninus Pius reveal that his two adopted sons, Marcus and Lucius, while no doubt close to the throne, were not associated with him in official titulature and would thus have been excluded from the address. Finally, Justin fails to salute Marcus Aurelius as Caesar, a title which he was given at least ten years prior to the composition of Justin's *Apology*.

Buck[22] also finds problems of form with *2 Apology*:

The address, 'To the Roman Senate,' … seems totally unrelated to the rest of the *Apology* … the confusion increases in that Justin invokes a single emperor in 2.8, yet in 2.16 he suggests that both Antoninus Pius and Marcus Aurelius are in power, and in both 14.1 and 15.2 he invokes more than one emperor.

As Roman citizens far less educated than Justin could and did petition the emperor with accurate and appropriate *petitio* Justin is without excuse for failing to observe the appropriate forms of address. On the basis of such irregularities, as well as the fact that both *Apologies* are overly lengthy, contain too many digressions and are contumacious in tone, Buck concludes that "(i)t is hardly likely, then, that Justin intended his *Apologies* to be read and considered by the imperial court,"[23] and "since his defences were not intended to be delivered before the emperor, Justin was not bound by official protocol and consciously defied it."[24] Why such conscious defiance by Justin? To serve a

---

22 Buck, "Justin Martyr's *Apologies*," pp. 52-53.
23 Buck, p. 55.
24 Buck, p. 56.

rhetorical purpose, namely, as a "bold attack upon the emperors, whose powers were unlimited, whose motives were self-serving, whose actions were irrational and whose reputations were as false as Justin's address."[25] In other words, Justin's intention was to sarcastically challenge, rather than defend, the emperors' right to their noble titles before the general public and his fellow Christians.

Other scholars also advocate a non-imperial destination for the *Apologies*. Rokéah[26] says that Justin addressed *1 Apology* to the Emperor Antoninus Pius and his adopted sons, "but his real audience was undoubtedly the pagan public in general." Wagner[27] contends that none of Justin's extant works were intended for those to whom they were formally addressed, "but were in-school models prepared by the master teacher to use by his students." Justin's students would study the form and content of his works to learn both the techniques of rhetoric and philosophy as well as their teacher's theology. On the other hand, both Frith[28] and Frend[29] believe that the *Apologies* were at least indirectly destined for the emperors and senate as they were distributed to the public as open letters to the Roman government.

Overall, on the basis of their length, form and the legal status of the Christians Justin most probably composed his *Apologies* in petition form to be publicly distributed as open letters to the government. The emperors were, therefore, only the "imaginary audience"[30]; the general pagan public and philosophically-

---

25 Buck, p. 57.

26 Rokéah, *Justin Martyr and the Jews*, p. 2.

27 Wagner, *Christianity in the Second Century*, p. 159.

28 F. Frith, "Saint Justin's Apologia," *Canadian Catholic Review* 7 (Nov. 1989), pp. 394-395 at p. 394.

29 W. H. C. Frend, *The Rise of Christianity*, Fortress, Philadelphia, 1984, p. 234.

30 Regarding the use of imaginary audiences by Christian writers, Mack, *Rhetoric and the New Testament*, p. 41, states, "the reader [is invited] to imagine an instance in which the proposition is actualized, even though the instance may be purely hypothetical, imaginary or idealistic."

minded were Justin's intended audience. Being open letters, Justin did not have to be so precise with his forms of address; nevertheless, he still included enough information in his titles to make clear that his message was ultimately for the emperors. The harsh language in both *1 Apology* and *2 Apology* was intended as a rhetorical device to highlight the judicial injustice being perpetrated against the Christians. Finally, Justin intended that Christians already in the Church would also use his *Apologies* for in-house catechetical, rhetorical and apologetical formation.

Considering these multiple destinations for his *Apologies*, what did Justin hope to achieve by writing to them? Purpose is essentially revealed through structure. By looking at structure one discerns progression and development, leading towards ultimate purposes.

According to Hardy[31], *1 Apology* reveals the following structure:

> (i) A plea that Christians receive a fair hearing (1-8).
> (ii) The faith and life of Christians (9-20).
> (iii) The superiority of Christianity over paganism (21-29).
> (iv) Arguments for Christ from prophecy (30-53).
> (v) The nature of Christian worship (61-67).
> (vi) Conclusion (68).

On the other hand, Justin himself provides some kind of schema in *1 Apol.* 23:

> (i) That what Christ and the prophets before him taught is alone true, and is teaching older than all other writers who have existed.
>
> (ii) That Jesus Christ is the only proper Son who has been begotten by God and taught us for the conversion and restoration of the human race.

---

31 E. R. Hardy, *Early Christian Fathers*, ed. C. C. Richardson, London, 1953, pp. 236-237.

And,

(iii) That pagan beliefs are fictitious and influenced by the demons, as are the scandalous reports against the Christians of infamous and impious actions.

Much shorter than *1 Apology*, *2 Apology* reveals the following structure:

(i) The recent injustice perpetrated by the Prefect Urbicus towards the Christians (1-3).
(ii) Why Christians did not just kill themselves if they were so intent on martyrdom (4).
(iii) Why the Christian God did not intervene to save them (5).
(iv) Divine providence, eternal punishment, the superiority of Christ, the Christian attitude towards death, request for publication, appeal for justice (6-15).

At this point it can be said that Justin aimed to persuade his pagan readers that the emperors should grant due process and toleration to the Christians through a forensic refutation of the three charges of atheism, immorality and disloyalty and positive comment about what Christians actually believed about God, behaviour and loyalty to the state. However, in both *Apologies* much of Justin's remaining material deals with God and Christ and its relationship to due process and the three charges is not immediately clear. He drifts from argument to exposition, from apologetics to catechetics. These meanderings make determining Justin's structure that much more difficult. However, Keresztes[32] provides some form of solution in the case of *1 Apology* through a collating of Justin's arguments into four groups (plus *peroration*) together with an examination of their rhetorical nature:

––––––––––––––

32 Keresztes, "The Literary Genre," pp. 101ff.

(i)   In *1 Apol.* 5-6 Justin puts forth the thesis that the Christian worship of the true God is superior to the pagan worship of false deities. This thesis becomes deliberative, protreptic rhetoric when Justin advises his readers to ensure that Christians are only charged and tried for crimes and not on the basis of their Christianity (*1 Apol.* 7, 8). It is also a protreptic argument when Justin argues that the adoption of Christianity would be more profitable to the state and the emperor by making the people of the empire better citizens. In *1 Apology* 9-12 Justin provides a refutation of the charges of atheism, non-participation in the official religion and disloyalty along the lines of forensic rhetoric.

(ii)   Justin's second group of arguments is an *apodeixis* demonstrating the parallel between certain teachings of Christ and those of pagan authorities (*argumentum de similibus*). Christian teachings on moral conduct (*1 Apol.* 14-17) eschatology (*1 Apol.* 18-20) and the birth, passion and resurrection of Christ (*1 Apol.* 20-22) are favourably compared to pagan beliefs on the same subjects. Justin puts this argument forward to support his demand that Christians at trials be examined for crimes other than Christianity.

(iii)   Justin's third group of arguments concerns the uniqueness of Christ and the superiority of Christian teachings over those of paganism (*argumenta a minori ad maius*). The thesis of Christ's uniqueness as the Son of God becomes a *suasoria*, or advice, seeking to achieve the deliberative-protreptic aim of moving his readers to heed the demand for judicial justice or face judgement and punishment from the hands of Christ (*1 Apol.* 45). The thesis of the superiority of

Christian teachings (*1 Apol.* 54-60) similarly becomes a *suasoria* supporting Justin's demand for justice for the Christians.

(iv) Justin's fourth group of arguments is again a thesis-cum-*suasoria* arguing that the Christian mysteries are innocent celebrations actually superior to pagan rites, the latter being mere imitations inspired by the demons (*1 Apol.* 61-67). It is provided as further support for the demand for judicial justice.

(v) The last chapter (*1 Apol.* 68) contains the *peroration* recalling the propositions made in the opening chapters, which followed the Apology's *exordium:* the Christians and their teachings may be honoured or despised but they should not be treated as public enemies or sentenced to death simply for confession of the Christian name without proof of any crimes being committed by them.

For Justin, emancipation would have been a great victory in the historic fight against the demons that sought control of the universe and of humanity. If the emperors were truly pious philosophers, they should not be flattered by ignorant and superstitious men to the point of allowing the condemnation of Christians solely on account of their name. When formally accused, Christians should be examined with respect to alleged *flagitia* and, if found guilty of any crime, be punished accordingly, but set free if found innocent (*1 Apol.* 2). Justin was confident that no true Christian could be guilty of serious wrongdoing.

Among scholars there is general agreement about Justin's desire for due process and toleration but disagreement as to whether the *Apologies* also harboured a deliberative missionary intention towards his pagan addressees. In the view of

Keresztes[33], Justin only wrote *1 Apology* to end the judicial injustices being perpetrated against Christians throughout the empire. This was tantamount to more than just social acceptance; it included also liberty of opinion and the emancipation of the Christian name.[34] Concerning Justin's calls to conversion (that is, inviting the emperor to pursue the "Christian philosophy"), Keresztes downplays such as mere protreptic rhetorical devices serving the more realistic purpose of influencing a change in judicial policy and practice in Asia.

Guerra[35] dismisses Keresztes' reasoning as unconvincing, positing the argument that because Justin extolled Christ and his teachings so extensively his primary aim must have been the conversion of the emperors (i.e., pagan addressees) to Christianity as the "true philosophy." According to him, Justin is relentless in his drive to lead the emperors to a higher form of piety (εὐσέβεια) and philosophy (φιλοσοφία), meaning Christianity.[36] Cosgrove calls this Justin's "evangelistic edge."[37] This was not merely for their salvation as individuals (*1 Apol.* 68; *2 Apol.* 15), but for greater strategic ends. Guerra[38] goes on to state that Justin was aware that "the emperor's conversion would

---

33 Keresztes, "Law and Arbitrariness," p. 211. The same author postulates in another article ("Literary Genre," p. 106) that Justin had in mind "special" trials in Asia initiated by mobs or cliques (without a specific denouncer) that had become a wide and persistent abuse.

34 Keresztes, "Law and Arbitrariness," p. 211; Goodenough, *The Theology of Justin Martyr*, p. 111, says, "It is not toleration but recognition which he demands, and it is to instill conviction of the moral and metaphysical truth of Christianity that he is striving."

35 Guerra, "The Conversion of Marcus Aurelius," p. 175.

36 For example, Justin, *1 Apol.* 16: "He has exhorted us to lead all people, by patience and gentleness, from shame and evil desires." This, while stressing the ability of Christianity to accept all that is true in pagan philosophy while rejecting the errors: Sikora, "Philosophy and Christian Wisdom," p. 253.

37 H. Cosgrove, "Justin Martyr and the Emerging Christian Canon," *Vigiliae Christianae* 36 (1982), pp. 209-232 at p. 211. For example, *1 Apol.* 10, 12, 13, 14, 16, 21, 23, 25, 40, 44, 53, 55.

38 Guerra, "The Conversion of Marcus Aurelius," p. 175.

open the way for the masses of pagans to accept Christianity, as well as concomitantly to end state persecution of Christians."

Skarsaune[39] would concur with Guerra, focussing on what he believes was Justin's concept of the task of the philosopher: "The proper task of philosophy is to reveal the true nature of the demons (pretending to be gods) and to bring men to the only true God." The philosopher, therefore, took a stand in the cosmic battle between the *Logos* and the demons. In Justin's case, he joined the battle to turn the emperors from idolatry to the God of Jesus Christ (*1 Apol.* 25). This battle exposed the true philosopher as a potential martyr, a potential Socrates, who was unjustly accused of atheism: "among the Greeks, Socrates and Heraclitus, and people like them" (*1 Apol.* 46). Justin was likewise willing to be reckoned among these 'atheists' in the cause of denouncing idolatry and defeating the demons.

In response to the charges that Christianity was philosophically and morally contemptible, Justin endeavoured to establish its essential rationality and its right to ownership to the glimpses of truth in philosophy (*2 Apol.* 13).[40] Not only was Christianity rational but also only in Christianity was the end of philosophy to be found. Once informed of its beliefs, the pagan addressees would see the superiority of the Christian religion (*1 Apol.* 23) and how it offered a deeper meaning and fuller content to the central terms of philosophy.[41] Following this, they would realise how Christianity would produce for the state better citizens (*1 Apol.* 12) and bring benefaction for the empire as a whole, leading them to concede the need to grant full emancipation and

39 Skarsaune, "The Conversion of Justin Martyr," p. 64.

40 R. Holte, "Logos Spermatikos: Christianity and Ancient Philosophy according to St. Justin's Apologies," *Studia Theologica* 12 (1958), pp. 109-168 at p. 113; A. J. Droge, "Justin Martyr and the Restoration of Philosophy," *Church History* 56 (1987), pp. 303-319 at p. 315.

41 J. L. Marshall, "Some observations on Justin Martyr's use of Testimonies," *Studia Patristica* 16/2 (1985), pp. 197-200 at p. 198.

eventually adopt Christianity themselves. The benefits flowing personally to the addressees from conversion would include the attainment of peace and happiness in the present life, freedom from being unwitting dupes of the invisible demons, and escape from eternal fire in the next (*1 Apol.* 17).

Justin's intention to convert his pagan addressees can also be surmised from his "proof from prophecy" argument. His in-depth outline of 'fulfilled prophecy' (chapters 32-53) could have served two purposes: as an *apodeixis* demonstrating the uniqueness of Jesus of Nazareth in support of the demand for emancipation; and/or to influence the wider public through the form of the emperors to consider Christianity. One who has been persuaded as to the supernatural value of a prophecy has taken a significant step towards acknowledging the supernatural nature of the religion that "owns" that prophecy. Justin appreciated this natural succession and aimed to achieve it in his pagan addressees, as evidenced at the end of chapter 53:

> Such things as these, then, when they are seen are sufficient to implant conviction and faith in those who welcome the truth, and are not vainglorious nor governed by their passions.

In summary, it can be asserted that through his *Apologies* Justin aimed to achieve the following apologetical purposes (in order of importance):

(i) To end the arbitrary injustices committed by the Roman judicial procedure against Christians for simply bearing the Christian name, and to save lives. Christians who have done nothing "contrary to the laws" should be free to live without interference. This Justin hoped to achieve by establishing the innocence of the Christians in the eyes of the general public, and through them to the emperors, against the charges of atheism, immorality and disloyalty that caused many pagans to blame the Christians for social conflicts and natural disasters that afflicted the empire.

(ii) To overcome ignorance and prejudice and to show forth Christianity's rationality through an unabridged presentation of Christian doctrines and practices and to recommend it to his pagan addressees as the only safe and useful philosophy and so ultimately win their adherence, or to at least enlist public sympathy and support for an end to arbitrary injustice.

(iii) To challenge the emperors' right to their noble titles before the general public and his fellow Christians.

(iv) To provide a useful catechetical, rhetorical and apologetical sourcebook for those already converted to Christianity, with the aim of fortifying such readers in their faith in Jesus of Nazareth as the promised messiah and to help them debate/convert pagans and heretics.

Destination and purpose of Dialogue with Trypho

Jurgens[42] offers the opinion that Justin wrote *Dialogue* c. AD 155. Quasten[43] gives the date for the composition of *Dialogue* as after AD 161. Most probably, Justin wrote *Dialogue* subsequent to both his *Apologies* and while living in Ephesus, where, according to Eusebius[44], he retired as a matter of prudence after publishing *2 Apology*.

Dialogue is a much later record of a two-day conversation

42 Jurgens, *The Faith of the Early Fathers*, pp. 50, 57, 58.
43 Quasten, *Patrology*, vol. 1, p. 199.
44 Eusebius, *History of the Church*, 4.18.6.

between Justin and a group of young Jewish men, including the learned Trypho, which took place in Ephesus between AD 132-135. Opinions differ as to the accuracy of Justin's account of the original conversation. Wagner[45] believes that *Dialogue* is "too long and literary" to be accurate. Osborn[46] in similar tones says, "There is too much dramatic and literary finesse for the conversation to be merely the result of a good memory."[47] Undoubtedly, Justin did engage in an extensive conversation with a learned Jew soon after his conversion but that *Dialogue* is a written account compiled decades after and embellished for his apologetic and proselytising purposes. As for Trypho, Goodenough[48] says that he was a Jew "who embodies the best of both schools of Judaism, one who knows Scripture and the Rabbinic interpretations ... and yet who has all the open-mindedness and cosmic sense of the Hellenistic Jews." Trypho's Judaism was, in the words of Barnard,[49] "a mediating Judaism" between the Judaism of the Pharisees and that of the extreme hellenisers.

Who were Justin's intended readers of *Dialogue*? The traditional view is that Justin intended *Dialogue* directly for the Jewish community as a defence of Christianity.[50] Chadwick[51] adds that Justin also intended it for Hellenised, liberalising Jews. However, Harnack rejects a Jewish destination, stating of *Dialogue*, "... what purports to be a polemic is nothing but

---

45 Wagner, *Christianity in the Second Century*, p. 263.

46 Osborn, *Justin Martyr*, p. 7.

47 Cf. G. N. Stanton, "Justin Martyr's Dialogue with Trypho: Group Boundaries, 'Proselytes' and 'God-fearers,'" in *Tolerance and Intolerance in Early Judaism and Christianity*, G. N. Stanton and G. G. Stroumsa, eds, Cambridge University Press, 1998, p. 263.

48 Goodenough, *The Theology of Justin Martyr*, p. 95.

49 Barnard, *St. Justin Martyr*, p. 25.

50 Barnard, *Justin Martyr: His Life and Thought*, pp. 21-26 and 170; W. A. Shotwell, *The Biblical Exegesis of Justin Martyr*, S.P.C.K., London, 1965, p. 2.

51 Chadwick, "Justin Martyr's Defence," p. 278.

apologetics for the internal use of the Church."[52] Rokéah[53] has recently resurrected a Jewish destination, maintaining that *Dialogue* was "intended for the Jews," due to its "friendly tone."

Stanton[54] offers the opinion that Justin intended *Dialogue* for unattached Gentiles who were broadly sympathetic to both Judaism and Christianity, yet unaware of the differences between them. Nilson[55] expresses an identical opinion. The preoccupation with the Old Testament leaves open the possibility of Stylianopoulos' view, that Justin certainly directed *Dialogue* to Jews and Christians simultaneously (with specific arguments and phrases directed against the followers of Marcion).[56] Wilson[57] argues in favour of the same dual destination, stating that Justin saw a need to immunise Christians against Jewish propaganda while at the same time seeking to convert Jews to Christianity.

As with the *Apologies*, an analysis of *Dialogue's* structure will assist in discerning Justin's intended audience and purpose(s). Justin's *Dialogue* reveals the following structure:

(i)   Justin's philosophical journey and conversion (1-9).

(ii)   The abrogation of the Mosaic Law (10-30).

(iii) Old Testament prophecies concerning Christ (31-108).

(iv)   On the superiority of the Christians as the "New Israel" and the conversion of the nations (109-141).

(v)   Conclusion and wishes for conversion of the Jews (142).

---

52 Quoted by D. Rokéah, *Jews, Pagans and Christians in Conflict*, The Magnes Press, Jerusalem, 1982, pp. 46-47.

53 Rokéah, *Jews, Pagans and Christians in Conflict*, p. 66. See also, Rokéah, *Justin Martyr and the Jews*, p. 9.

54 Stanton, "Justin Martyr's Dialogue with Trypho," p. 275.

55 Nilson, "To whom is Justin's *Dialogue with Trypho* Addressed?," p. 539.

56 Stylianopoulos, *Justin Martyr and the Mosaic Law*, pp. 25-32 & 36.

57 S. G. Wilson, *Related Strangers: Jews and Christians 70-170 CE*, Fortress Press, Minneapolis, 1995, pp. 261-265.

The *Dialogue's* structure reveals that Justin's mind was concerned with various deliberative and educational purposes, namely, the absolute need for conversion, giving direction to potential converts as to how Christians should live and practise as distinct from Jews, emphasising the continued relevance and importance of the Old Testament for Christians, and reinforcing those who were already 'on the inside' by highlighting their special and superior status with God.

As a philosopher and Christian Justin's constant theme was love of truth.[58] Therefore, according to Osborn[59], he "wanted to show why he had become a Christian by explaining how it had happened ... He did all this because he wanted others to follow him to the only safe and useful philosophy." Sikora[60] similarly states that Justin was motivated by a basic desire to share his discovery of the 'true philosophy' with others and to help others find the God of the Christians, as witnessed by Justin's statement: "Moreover, I would wish that *all* [italics added], making a resolution similar to my own, do not keep themselves away from the words of the Saviour" (*Dial.* 8). Rokéah also likens Justin to a missionary propagandist, seeking not only to clear up misunderstandings and superstitions "which lead the reader only to the door of the Church," but also opening the door and ushering him "into the Church's inner sanctum."[61] In other words, he sought no less than the deliberative objective of conversion to Christianity. This is evidenced by the fact that Justin "does not limit himself to defending Christianity against the attacks ... but broadens his scope to include a presentation

58 E. F. Osborn, "Justin Martyr and the Logos Spermatikos," *Studia Missionalia* 42 (1993), pp. 143-159 at 147; Osborn, *Justin Martyr*, p. 77, states, "Justin's love of truth dominates his life. He declares he would die rather than deny what is true."
59 Osborn, *Justin Martyr*, p. 67.
60 Sikora, "Philosophy and Christian Wisdom," p. 255.
61 Rokéah, *Justin Martyr and the Jews*, p. 3.

of Scripture as the foundation of the Gospels."[62]

Horbury[63] believes that Justin wrote out of the Church's "need to affirm itself over against the larger and more powerful Jewish community." Cosgrove[64] imagines that it certainly served as a helpful internal sourcebook for study by Christians for apology to Jews, but argues that *Dialogue*'s preoccupation with the Old Testament indicates that Justin most likely intended internal use to combat the threat of Marcion and the foisting of law-keeping on Gentile Christians in Rome.[65] However, such a preoccupation with the Old Testament would also be unavoidable if *Dialogue* was intended primarily for a Jewish audience. At the same time extensive focus on the Old Testament (for the purpose of vindicating the New Testament) could not be avoided if—as Stanton and Nilson argue—Justin wrote *Dialogue* to convert unattached Gentiles considering a choice between Judaism and Christianity.[66]

In recent times, two other scholars, Mach and Setzer, have expressly rejected any idea that Justin's *Dialogue* harboured a deliberative missionary intent directed towards the Jews. Mach considers *Dialogue* "… mainly as a document of an intra-Christian process … Justin had one eye directed to the pagan audience and the other to his own Christian community."[67] Hints of missionary action directed at Jews are "… at most,

---

62 Ibid.

63 W. Horbury, *Jews and Christians in Contact and Controversy*, T & T Clark, Edinburgh, 1998, p. 23.

64 Cosgrove, "Emerging Christian Canon," p. 219.

65 Chadwick, "Justin Martyr's Defence," p. 290, gives one persuasive reason for Justin's extensive use of Old Testament quotes, namely, to oppose Marcion's rejection of the Old Testament, a rejection that undermined his argument from prophecy and threatened to destroy his "entire conception of the divine activity in and through history."

66 Stanton, "Justin Martyr's Dialogue with Trypho," p. 275.

67 M. Mach, "Justin Martyr's *Dialogus cum Tryphone Iudaeo* and the Development of Christian Anti-Judaism," in O. Limor and G. G. Stroumsa, eds., *Contra Iudaeos: Ancient and Medieval Polemics between Christians and Jews*, J. C. B. Mohr, Tübingen, 1996, pp. 30 and 47.

marginal comments."[68] Setzer argues for the same conclusion, believing that if Justin intended to convert Jews he would have had Trypho admit the superiority of his arguments and convert by the end of the work.[69]

In Setzer's view, the purpose of *Dialogue* was to challenge Marcionite rejection of the Torah, and to preserve its authority as it attested to Jesus and the truths of Christianity. However, as Rokéah[70] observes, Justin "… did this, however, in his *Syntagma*, whereas the Marcionites receive only scant regard in the *Dialogue*." Concerning Mach, Rokéah asks, "What is the basis for Mach's argument?"[71] The answer is, very little. Mach relies on the same point made by Setzer—that, "Trypho remains a faithful Jew throughout the *Dialogue*, does not accept baptism nor indicates that he will in the future." The following response can be given to both Mach and Setzer: Justin's work was intended mainly for intra-Christian purposes and unattached pagans but is not purely a work of fiction. Rather, as stated earlier, it is a written account of an historic conversation, though significantly embellished for apologetic and proselytising purposes. At the time Justin tried his utmost to convert Trypho and his companions using the best-developed arguments known to him; nevertheless, Trypho still chose not to convert, though he acknowledges the persuasiveness of Justin's arguments at various points (*Dial.* 60, 63, 89, 94). Justin is honest enough to report the dialogue truthfully and shrewd enough to use it to illustrate what he considered the unreasonable obstinacy of the Jews. Justin assumed that if he could repeat the same arguments to Christians and unprejudiced pagans they would be either fortified in, or convinced enough to embrace, Christianity.

---

68 Rokéah, *Justin Martyr and the Jews*, p. 14.
69 C. J. Setzer, *Jewish Responses to Early Christian History and Polemics, 30-150 CE*, Fortress Press, Minneapolis, 1994, pp. 129, 133, 135-138, 146.
70 Rokéah, *Justin Martyr and the Jews*, p. 14, n. 13.
71 Rokéah, *Justin Martyr and the Jews*, p. 14.

Lieu[72] reviews the arguments relating to destination and purpose, and provides a cautious opinion of her own, one which harmonises well its various ends:

> The discussion has shown that it is dangerous to posit too exclusive alternatives. Internal Christian concerns have shaped Justin's sources as well as his present argument; a tradition of missionary concern which included those who might equally be attracted by Judaism can also not be excluded; sympathetic pagans might be swayed by some of the arguments.

Ultimately, it can be said that Justin did not intend *Dialogue* to be handed immediately to or read by Jews but rather intended it for the following simultaneous non-Jewish destinations:

(i)   For unattached Gentiles (God-fearers).

(ii) For internal use by Christians.

The reasons for believing that Justin intended such destinations only are:

(i)   The name "Marcus Pompeius" (mentioned in chs. 8 and 141) suggests an addressee who was more likely a Roman Gentile.

(ii) The reference to "those who wish to become converts" in chapter 23 could hardly be to Trypho and his companions as they were committed Jews.

(iii) The literary style of *Dialogue* which reflects that of Socratic dialogue suggests an educated pagan audience.

(iv) *Dialogue's* lengthy and intense focus on Old Testament prophecy suggests that it was a response to an internal need to catechise and fortify the local Roman Christian community.

---

72 J. M. Lieu, *Image and Reality: The Jews in the World of the Christians in the Second Century*, T & T Clark, Edinburgh, 1996, p. 108.

(v)   Justin's uncompromising attacks against circumcision, Jewish teachers and the Jewish claim to be faithful interpreters of Scripture points to an intended audience of Gentile proselytes attracted to Judaism but still open to persuasion.

(vi)   *Dialogue*'s prolixity, strident tone of language and severe portrayal of the Jews (for example, *Dial.* 32, 39, 44, 55, 64, 68, 92, 110, 134) lends itself to being a document intended for long-term study by those who would not feel implicated by its contents rather than for a people who would have found significant portions of it offensive.

(vii)   The Jews would have been offended by Justin's choice of an interlocutor as inadequate as Trypho and for reducing much of the conversation with him to a monologue.

Furthermore, it can be concluded that Justin wrote *Dialogue* to achieve the following deliberative and/or educational purposes:

(i)   He wanted others to know of and follow him into the "only safe and useful philosophy," namely Christianity, that is, to convert unattached Gentiles who were broadly sympathetic to both Judaism and Christianity. *Dialogue*'s length, strident tone and polemic evidences that it was written against the Jews, but not to them or for them. Hints of missionary action directed at Jews are at most, marginal comments, illustrative only of a general desire that they convert to Christ.

(ii)   To provide a helpful internal sourcebook for study by Christians for apology to Jews. Christians encountering members of the sizeable Jewish community in Rome needed intense formation in and knowledge of the Old Testament and how it related to Christ. Christians needed apologetics not simply to defend their beliefs against well-educated Jews but to engage in an urgent proselytism to save as many of them as possible before the soon arriving Last Judgement.

(iii) To combat Judaising Christians who wished to foist law-keeping on Gentile Christians in Rome. That is, to provide a concrete Christian self-definition. While retaining the Old Testament, there developed the need to distinguish the ceremonial from the moral precepts of the Law and to explain why the former were now abrogated for Christians.

(iv) To counter Marcion and his rejection of the Torah. The strength of Marcion's schism during Justin's time in Rome urged a re-affirmation of Christian belief in both the Jewish God and the Old Testament Scriptures as well as a more developed defence of Christian reverence yet non-observance of the Jewish Law. This defence would go hand-in-hand with anti-Jewish polemic.

To conclude that Justin composed *Dialogue* for multiple purposes is in line with the bulk of modern scholarship on *adversus Iudaeos* literature. According to Stroumsa[73]:

Polemics, then, is the literary reflection of the conflictual relationship between competing religious groups. But it serves multiple purposes. It does not intend only, or even mainly, to convince and

---

73 G. Stroumsa, "From Anti-Judaism to Antisemitism in Early Christianity?" in O. Limor and G. G. Stroumsa (eds), *Contra Iudaeos: Ancient and Medieval Polemics between Christians and Jews*, Texts and Studies in Medieval and Early Modern Judaism 10, J. C. B. Mohr, Tübingen, 1996, pp. 1-26 at p. 18.

convert, but also to strengthen the faith, or the self-confidence, of those who are already converted. Polemics, indeed, serves as a major tool in group-identity building and affirming.

Despite his various purposes, the basic strategies of Justin's *Dialogue* remained the same: to establish continuity between Judaism and Christianity, to represent Christianity as the fulfilment of the mystical and ancient books of the Old Testament, and to find in the Old Testament prophetic descriptions of the person and work of Christ. All this was in order that his reader "may be of the same opinion as ourselves, and believe that Jesus is the Christ of God" (*Dial.* 142).

Chapter 5

Justin's Apologetical Arguments in *1* and *2 Apology*

In the previous chapter, I concluded that Justin published his *Apologies* as open letters to the government, for distribution among the general public and philosophically-minded, and for in-house use among Christians to achieve the following purposes:

(1) To end the arbitrary injustices committed by the Roman judicial procedure against Christians by establishing the latter's innocence in the eyes of the general public and philosophically-minded, and through them to the emperors, against the charges of atheism, immorality and disloyalty.

(2) To overcome ignorance and prejudice and to show forth Christianity's rationality through an unabridged presentation of Christian doctrines and practices and to recommend it to his pagan addressees as the only safe and useful philosophy and so ultimately win their adherence, or to at least enlist public sympathy and support for an end to arbitrary injustice.

(3) To challenge the emperors' right to their noble titles before the general public and his fellow Christians.

(4) To provide a useful catechetical, rhetorical and apologetical sourcebook for those already converted to Christianity.

Justin's task was immense, and to have any hope of success he needed to formulate and present an array of arguments that simultaneously met the objections and attacks of the hostile and answered clearly and persuasively the questions of the curious. In this chapter, Justin's most outstanding arguments in both *1* and *2 Apology* are selected, summarised and analysed as to their nature and appropriateness. As stated at the beginning of this study, by 'appropriate' is meant 'suitable' or 'proper' taking into account the rhetorical and literary conventions of second-century Graeco-Roman culture, the contemporary social situation, Justin's intended audience and his purpose. Would Justin's arguments from the point of view of second-century standards have been reasonable, possessing at least a potential for effectiveness, or would they have been dismissed without serious consideration, or even worsened the plight of Christians?

For the sake of clarity the relevant purpose and audience will first be listed before commencing the detailed outline and assessment of each of Justin's arguments. The same process will be followed for *Dialogue* in Chapter 6.

The Argument from Behaviour

Purpose: To establish Christian innocence against the charges of atheism, immorality and disloyalty

As outlined in Chapter 3, the plight of second-century Christians was exacerbated by the numerous allegations of immoral behaviour that were circulated against them. These accusations were spread through popular gossip and included, in particular, sexual debauchery, ritual murder, cannibalism, impiety, atheism, and disloyalty. Their dissemination periodically incited mob violence and triggered renewed persecution by local magistrates and governors. Even before his conversion Justin was aware of these allegations in detail (*1 Apol.* 5-12) and sought to rebut them.[74] He might well have believed that detailed descriptions of Christian moral teachings, ritual worship, and their everyday lives were more likely to impress the emperors and achieve his protreptic purpose of securing a change of judicial behaviour than any presentation of Christianity as a philosophy.

With "confident simplicity"[75] Justin outlined the moral character of Christianity in quotations and phrases from the Scriptures scattered throughout the *Apologies.* He gave examples of Christ's teachings— mostly from the Sermon on the Mount— —concerning purity, temperance, patience and generosity (*1 Apol.* 15, 16). Justin without hesitation proclaimed to the emperors that Christians, following the injunctions of Jesus, renounced all forms of lust, adultery and divorce so as to practise perfect chastity: "And many, both men and women, who have been Christ's disciples from childhood, have preserved their purity at the age of sixty or seventy years; and I am proud that I could produce such from every race of men and women" (*1 Apol.* 15). Justin boasted that, in contrast to pagans who married for lust and exposed their offspring, Christians married to bring up children (*1 Apol.* 39), and that Christ even called some to renounce all forms of sexual activity for the sake of the kingdom of heaven (*1 Apol.* 15). The moral integrity of Christians was further evidenced by their willingness to die as martyrs when they could have easily escaped torture and death through deceit or retraction (*1 Apol.* 8, 39; *2 Apol.* 4).

Justin's forensic purpose was to lift the "wicked disguise which the evil demons had cast over the divine doctrines of the

---

74 It was witnessing Christians who endured suffering and martyrdom under fierce persecution that first prompted Justin to give consideration to their opinions. See Osborn, "Justin's Response," p. 46. Justin concluded that such courage was impossible if the allegations of immorality levelled against them were true. For how could sensual and immoral persons put moral and rational values above life itself?

75 Martindale, C. C., *St. Justin the Martyr,* Harding and More, London, 1921, p. 36.

Christians" (*2 Apol.* 13), which he believed deterred others from joining them and gave persecution its excuse. As the demons hated those pagans who lived according to partial truth[76], it followed for Justin that they hated even more those who lived by the whole truth. If the emperors were made to realise that Christians were in fact innocent of immorality, then they would feel compelled legally to protect them from mob violence and arbitrary justice.

Justin believed that the differences between pagan and Christian behaviour stemmed largely from the work of the demons. Justin refers to the demons as the source of wickedness in at least twelve chapters in *1 Apology*, the most notable being in chapters 5, 12, 14, 21, 23, 26, 28 and 58. The demons effected terrifying apparitions of themselves in order to subjugate humanity and to cause the pagans to give them divine honours and worship (*1 Apol.* 5, 12, 14, 25, 62). They possessed a mental hold over pagan humanity through dreams, magic, myths, poets and idolatry, and inspired falsehood as much as the *Logos* inspired truth. The demons continued to afflict humanity as a whole, dominating, corrupting and interfering in its affairs (*2 Apol.* 5, 12). Christians, on the other hand, denied worship to the pagan gods, recognising them for what they really were— demons (*1 Apol.* 9).[77] Furthermore, upon learning of the truths and prophecies found in Scripture, the demons, through the

---

76 According to R. M. Price, "Are there 'Holy Pagans' in Justin Martyr?," *Studia Patristica* 31 (1997), pp. 167-171 at p. 170, Justin supposed that pagans "antagonized the demons not simply by virtuous living but by monotheism and opposition to idolatry." This is best evidenced by Justin's commendation of Socrates as one persecuted and put to death for "introducing new divinities" in opposition to the established iniquity (*1 Apol.* 5).

77 Goodenough, *The Theology of Justin Martyr*, p. 109, states that the belief that the gods of pagan mythology were "wicked and impious demons" is "so far as we know first suggested in Christian literature by Justin." For pagans, demons were baneful creatures but distinct and less powerful than the gods according to R. MacMullen, *Christianizing the Roman Empire*, Yale University Press, New Haven and London, 1984, p. 13. Martindale, *St. Justin the Martyr*, p. 133, notes that other pagans propounded a so-called "Euhemerist theory," i.e., "that the gods were really men, glorified by the imagination of succeeding centuries."

agency of poets, promoted imitations of Christian beliefs to pre-empt and subvert the spread of Christianity (*1 Apol.* 54, 56). The demons also busily inspired mimicries of Christian rituals such as baptism (*1 Apol.* 62, 64, 66), and spawned heretics such as Simon, Menander and Marcion (*1 Apol.* 25).

Justin protested the innocence of Christians against the charges of disloyalty by asserting that they gladly served and prayed for the emperor and, in accordance with Christ's own exhortations, "more readily than all people [pay] the taxes and assessments" (*1 Apol.* 17). Christians did not seek a human kingdom in opposition to the empire, but one "of God" (*1 Apol.* 11). A "countless multitude" by converting to Christianity had reformed intemperate habits, renounced worldly treasures, and adopted in their stead love, kindness and charity towards their enemies and the needy (*1 Apol.* 15). Such behaviour, Justin complained, was scarcely treasonable (*1 Apol.* 11, 12, 16, 17, 27), but rather transformed the whole structure of personal, social, and political relationships to conform to generosity, integrity, and justice.

Accusations of immorality against Christians were often based on evils such as incestuous orgies and cannibalism said to be committed during their acts of corporate worship.[78] These allegations received popular acceptance due to the general ignorance about Christianity and the fact that Christians

---

78 The most noteworthy of these attacks was issued by the former consul, Marcus Cornelius Fronto (consul in AD 143; d. AD 166) in a speech delivered c. AD 157, quoted by Minucius Felix, *Octavius*, 9: "Assuredly this confederacy ought to be rooted out and execrated. They know one another by secret marks and insignia, and they love one another almost before they know one another. Everywhere also there is mingled among them a certain religion of lust, and they call one another promiscuously brothers and sisters, that even a not unusual debauchery may by the intervention of that sacred name become incestuous … I hear that they adore the head of an ass, that basest of creatures, consecrated by I know not what silly persuasion,—a worthy and appropriate religion for such manners. Some say that they worship the *virilia* of their pontiff and priest, and adore the nature, as it were, of their common parent …".

kept their corporate worship away from the public eye.[79] As the accusations were so gross and widespread, no change of state policy towards the Christians could be expected without a detailed explanation of Christian worship, and Justin was prepared to supply it. He systematically outlined the Christian's communal Sunday worship, and provided a detailed account of the administration and meaning of the Christian sacraments of baptism and the eucharist. Justin's conviction was that Christianity, being true, had nothing to fear from scrutiny, and that, far from being black magic, Christian rites were actually innocuous and morally uplifting. In so doing, Justin was one of the first to write publicly about the esoteric life of the Christian community, in contrast to the established custom known as the *disciplina arcani* (discipline of the secret), or doctrine of reserve.[80]

Justin presented Christian rituals as very simple and innocent (*1 Apol.* 61, 65-67),[81] with the artlessness of a simple member of the Church. He introduced his account almost incidentally to assure his readers that no horrors are perpetrated at Christian gatherings. In weekly communal worship, Christians simply read "the memoirs of the Apostles or the writings of the prophets," listened to the exhortation of the president, prayed for the Church and the world, offered each other the kiss of peace,

---

79 J. S. Romanides, "Justin Martyr and the Fourth Gospel," *The Greek Orthodox Theological Review* 4 (1958-1959), pp. 115-134 at p. 120, states that the fact that Christian mysteries "were not open to the general public and never discussed with the uninitiated needs no demonstration." Whereas Justin invites the authorities to look into Christian writings (*1 Apol.* 28), he nowhere invites the officials to attend the Christian gatherings to see for themselves.

80 According to Barnard, *St. Justin Martyr*, pp. 134-135, "Apart from the *Apostolic Tradition* of Hippolytus of Rome, Justin's account of the Christian sacraments of baptism and the Eucharist are the most detailed from pre-Nicene times."

81 Barnard, *St. Justin Martyr*, p. 130, states, "as a result of his evident desire to emphasise the simplicity of the Christian sacraments Justin does not give an accurate description of the officers of the Church or their relations to one another and the whole body of Christ."

celebrated the eucharist, and made offerings for the needy (*1 Apol.* 67). This worship was held on Sunday because that was the day on which Christ rose from the dead. The sermon of the president included both instruction and moral exhortation. The monies collected were distributed by the president for the benefit of widows, orphans, the sick, prisoners and others in need. This was *what* the Christians did and the *way* they did it.

Justin explained the rite of baptism as the formal rite of initiation for Christians, the next necessary step after "believe[ing] that the things we teach and say are true" (*1 Apol.* 61). It involved the convert being washed with water "in the name of God the Father and Master of all, and of our Saviour Jesus Christ, and of the Holy Spirit" (*1 Apol.* 61). This washing gave the convert a new birth into purity and knowledge (ἐjπιστήμη), a "remission of sins and for rebirth" (*1 Apol.* 66). Justin called the baptismal washing "illumination [φωτισμός], as those who learn these things are illuminated in the mind" (*1 Apol.* 61). Only after baptism was the new believer brought into the presence of the Christian congregation, to participate in the prayers and thanksgivings and to partake of the eucharist (*1 Apol.* 65).

As for the eucharist, Justin emphasised that it was not "common bread nor common drink" but rather "the flesh and blood of that Jesus who became incarnate" (*1 Apol.* 66). This change, explained Justin, was wrought by the words Jesus himself spoke over the bread and wine at the Last Supper and which he ordered his disciples to repeat (*1 Apol.* 66). According to Romanides[82], Justin made these comments "not for the purpose of convincing any pagans regarding the truth of the matter, but in order to refute the charge that 'we eat men' and to demonstrate the harmless nature of the Christian gatherings."

---

82 Romanides, "Justin Martyr and the Fourth Gospel," p. 120.

Not content simply with providing a detailed explanation of Christian worship, Justin resolved to argue in favour of the moral superiority of the Christian lifestyle over that of the pagan. Christians, he declared, were not only innocent of the charges raised against them; they were exemplary citizens, better than the average pagan. Pagan practices such as infant exposure, prostitution, sodomy and self-mutilation were not found among the Christians (*1 Apol.* 27). Such disparity, according to Justin, flowed from the nature of the respective deities worshipped, for the pagan deities were guilty of parricide, sodomy and adultery (*1 Apol.* 21, 25; *2 Apol.* 12), and "all consider it an honourable thing to imitate the gods" (*1 Apol.* 21). Justin intended to attract converts in the same way through which he and many others had been converted (*2 Apol.* 12), that is, by preparing the will through a presentation of the goodness, truth and beauty of the Christian God and lifestyle.

Appropriateness of the argument

Justin was aware that the Romans were a deeply religious people, but that Rome never sought to impose any single religious faith or worship, rather leaving undisturbed the religious beliefs of her subject peoples. Action was only taken against any new religion if it gave social, moral or political offence, as was the case with the Great Mother (*Magna Mater*) cult of Cybele in 204 BC and the suppression of the Bacchic cult in 186 BC. If Justin could convince his audience that Christianity did not engage in anything like the orgiastic licences and self-mutilation practised by the priests of Cybele, but rather was morally upright and peaceful, then certainly his application was well grounded and reasonable, consistent with the Roman practice of granting freedom to the followers of any religion that did not threaten others or the *pax Romana.*

Justin's appeal to the moral character (*ethos*) of Christians sought to create sympathy for their plight. Aristotle considered proofs based on *ethos* to be the most effective form of proof. The practical worth of Justin's presentation of the moral teachings and everyday lifestyle of the Christians lay in its potential to achieve two critical rhetorical objectives as well as one catechetical one: forensically, to nullify the calumnies spread through popular gossip and rumour of sexual debauchery, ritual murder, cannibalism, etc., for unless the government were made to see that Christian teachings and behaviour were not morally reprehensible then change was impossible; deliberatively, to turn the conscience of the better part of public opinion to view them favourably, deserving not only of due process and liberty of worship, but worthy of consideration as a religio-philosophical lifestyle beneficial to both individuals and the empire as a whole; and to provide a useful in-house handbook to strengthen converts in Christian morality, liturgical understanding and worship. Again, unless Justin's pagan addressees were confronted with Christian moral beliefs in their reality there was no possibility that they would grant licence to or adopt a belief system that was rumoured to practise only vices execrated by the prevailing philosophies of the time.

Justin's 'morality' rhetoric first sought to equate Christian morals with those of Stoicism, the philosophy of the emperors. Stoics (as well as Platonists and Cynics) strongly embraced certain ascetic principles. These included self-mastery, rational detachment and mental discipline, virtues considered essential for maintaining the moral and ideological backbone of the empire. In presenting Christian asceticism as espousing these same virtues Justin highlighted its value as a potential ally in the struggle for the empire's social well-being (particularly in an age of acknowledged moral decline). The same could equally be said for Justin's claim of Christian sexual purity. Since the time of

Augustus Caesar (27 BC - AD 14) the increasing levels of divorce, falling birth rates and sexual promiscuity were of continuous public concern at the highest levels.[83] Marriage and procreation were regarded as natural, patriotic and sacred duties (*pietates*) incumbent on Romans and humanity as a whole, and second-century Stoic philosophers such as Musonius Rufus, Hierocles, Epictetus and Antipater of Tarsus strenuously upheld the same while condemning extramarital sex, adultery, homosexuality and the exposure of infants. As Jesus' elevated norm of sexual purity outlined in *1 Apol.* 15 coincided with these Stoic sexual ideals and concerns it was certainly reasonable on Justin's part to believe that his *apodeixis* would have been both sympathetically received and persuasive among the philosophically-minded.

Philanthropy, or justice towards one's neighbour, was another highly valued virtue among the ancients.[84] It was believed that superstitious or impious men with their own private code of values were incapable of practising justice, engaging only in shameful practices to the detriment of the public good. As some defined Christianity as a depraved superstition it is understandable why Justin twice mentioned almsgiving as a regular practice of Christians (*1 Apol.* 15, 67). Justin's rationale rested on the belief that a demonstration of Christian philanthropy would prove that Christianity engendered virtues at least equal to, if not better than, other accepted philosophies. Justin's assumption was certainly not implausible, considering the observations of his contemporary, the philosopher-doctor Galen. Like other Greeks, Galen believed that there was a

---

83 H. Rhee, *Early Christian Literature: Christ and Culture in the Second and Third Centuries*, Routledge, London and New York, 2005, p. 109. Legislation designed to uphold a conservative ethic for marriage, family and social order included the *Lex Iulia de maritandis ordinibus* (18 BC) and the *Lex Papia Poppaea* (AD 9). Marcus Aurelius was particularly concerned with the issues of sexual purity and chastity: Guerra, "The Conversion of Marcus Aurelius," p. 180.
84 Cicero considered it the "queen of virtues" (*On the Nature of the Gods* 1.3).

strong connection between reasonable thinking and virtue. Galen encountered Christians and despite concluding that they were poor physicians was willing to accept Christianity as a philosophical school as it certainly led men to virtue.[85]

Christian philanthropy may have provided a powerful commendation to a society that certainly saw social relief as an urgent necessity. The Graeco-Roman world was replete with private voluntary associations (whether religious, philosophical, vocational, etc.) that sought to promote good living, right thinking and piety.[86] During times of rapid social change or upheaval such groups especially catered to the needs of their members when government or kinship groups failed. By outlining the voluntary nature of Christian membership, rules for entry, its formal organisation, and standards of behaviour, Justin laid the foundations for depicting Christianity as an eligible voluntary association.[87] Yet, the Romans were sometimes reticent to grant approval to new associations lest, in the words of Trajan, "the same become a political association before long."[88] As noted in Chapter 3, Christianity's 'exclusiveness' lent itself to the accusation of being clandestine and politically subversive. Therefore, Justin needed to provide evidence of how Christianity could publicly benefit the empire as a matter of absolute necessity. This need was not necessarily discharged by showing that the Christian "Presider" (*1 Apol.* 67) made the distribution of charitable monies and goods only to members of his own church. Nevertheless, there were still philosophical

---

85 R. L. Wilken, "Toward a Social Interpretation of Early Christian Apologetics," *Church History* 39 (1970), pp. 437-458 at p. 448.

86 S. G. Wilson, "Voluntary Associations: An Overview," in *Voluntary Associations in the Graeco-Roman World*, edd. J. S. Kloppenborg and S.G. Wilson, Routledge, London and New York, 1996, pp. 1-15 at p. 3.

87 W. O. McCready, "Ekklēsia and Voluntary Associations," in *Voluntary Associations in the Graeco-Roman World*, edd. J. S. Kloppenborg and S.G. Wilson, Routledge, London and New York, 1996, pp. 59-73 at p. 61.

88 Trajan, *Epistle* 10.33, 34.

communities that promoted an exclusive community of goods that operated with approval. Furthermore, it remained open to Justin to argue that the charitable banquets provided for local Christian communities by their wealthier members at least promoted a level of behaviour that contrasted favourably against the shenanigans committed at pagan banquets.[89]

However, one weakness in Justin's 'morality' rhetoric was his failure to actually provide demonstrable evidence that Christians followed the lofty teachings of their master. The need to do so was made more urgent by the fact that there were significant numbers who claimed the Christian name but, nevertheless, did not live up to it.[90] These rogue elements were sufficient in number to come to the notice of the general Roman population and undermine Justin's whole *ethos*, requiring Justin to respond that they were Christian in name only (*1 Apol.* 26). For the authorities, who had little way and even less interest in determining who were the real Christians, reports of the activities of the charlatans, etc., would have severely dented the credibility of Justin's idealised portrayal of Christian morality. To counter this, Justin could have extended an offer to the authorities to attend Christian gatherings to view their worship and lifestyle for themselves. Such an invitation may have left the positive impression that Justin had "nothing to hide" and was a

---

89 C. A. Bobertz, "The Role of Patron in the Cena Dominica of Hippolytus' Apostolic Tradition," *Journal of Theological Studies* 44 n.s. (1993), pp. 170-184 at p. 177. Bobertz provides an example of pagan behaviour at one banquet from the writings of Juvenal, who speaks of cheap wine converting the revellers into "corybants" as a prelude to foul words, flying tankards and crockery, and patrons leaving with bloody wounds.

90 Barnard, *St. Justin Martyr*, p. 156. Barnard asks whether the moral picture of Christians presented by Justin "is not too idealised," considering "that in any age there are many nominal Christians whose conduct and moral level is no different from that of the surrounding non-Christian population." Wilken, "Toward a Social Interpretation of Early Christian Apologetics," p. 442, states: "In many communities the bishops and teachers presided over an unruly lot of Christians … Christianity had its fair share of opportunists, charlatans, confidence men as well as the greedy, slothful, and perverse."

viable means of substantiating his morality claims. Realistically, though, extending such an invitation in Justin's time was impossible as he himself was not at liberty to invite outsiders in violation of the exclusive nature of this worship and any invitation would have exposed Christians to arrest by hostile Roman authorities. Nevertheless, Justin did draw support from the example of the martyrs, who by their voluntary sacrifices gave public evidence that there were enough Christians who certainly strove to live and die according to the ideal and their testimony emitted a living influence more impressive than any philosophical defence or argument. As Justin proclaimed,

> For no one trusted in Socrates so as to die for this doctrine, but in Christ ... not only philosophers and scholars believed, but also artisans and people entirely uneducated, despising both glory, and fear, and death; since he is a power of the ineffable Father, not the mere instrument of human reason (*2 Apol.* 10).

Justin's attacks against the moral decadence of much of pagan society initially would have received a sympathetic hearing from noble pagans who were likewise concerned. However, his assertion that the activity of the demons was responsible for much of pagan immorality would have been dismissed as overly simplistic and lacking in understanding of Graeco-Roman belief in daimonia (δαίμωνια). For while both Christians and pagans (including eminent philosophers of all the schools) believed that the spirit-world was a very real one the classical pagan understanding of "daimon" was far more expansive than the fixed Christian concept of "demon." Pagan daimons could either be individual gods or goddesses (Homer, *Iliad* 3.420), the superhuman impersonal force belonging to a god of some kind (the Latin *numen*), the power controlling the destiny of individuals, the good or evil genius of a person or family, the souls of the men of the golden age of Hesiod (Hesiod, *Op.* 121-126), general semi-divine creatures intermediate between gods and men (Plato, *Laws* 848D), or beings who associated with and ruled over an individual from birth and guided their soul after death (Plato, *Phaedo* 107D; Aristotle *Frg.* 193).[91] For pagans, the influence of daimons could be either good or bad depending on whether the person was under the influence of a εὐδαίμων (good daimon) or κακοδαίμων (evil daimon).[92] For the sake of credibility, Justin needed to exercise some caution and subtlety in his argument, avoiding any definition of "demon" that included all pagan daimons, whether good or bad, instead supplying a definition that clearly limited the meaning of demon solely to malevolent spiritual influences.

In any case, Justin's claim that virtually the whole of pagan civilisation was enslaved to the demons (meaning evil daimons) was one that would have been rejected as highly exaggerated. Justin did not limit demonic domination to a minority but implied that the whole of humanity was subject to them (*2 Apol.* 5). The only exceptions were individuals such as Socrates, Heraclitus or Musonius and others (*2 Apol.* 8). If Justin's petition achieved wide distribution among the public such a generalisation would have triggered the indignation of most noble or philosophical

---

91 John E. Rexine, "Daimon in Classical Greek Literature," *Greek Orthodox Theological Review*, 30 (1985), pp. 335-361 at p. 335. For a concise analysis of the various kinds of spirits believed by pagans in the Graeco-Roman world see also Georg Luck, *Arcana Mundi. Magic and the Occult in the Greek and Roman World*, John Hopkins University, Baltimore, 1985, pp. 163-175.

92 It was not until the Hellenistic period (323 BC – 146 BC) that daimons were considered to have either a fixed good or evil character. Evil daimons were manipulable by humans through invocations and magic and could be called upon to inflict misfortunes such as plagues, riots, disease, or to eliminate an enemy or inflame an unrequited love. They were also believed to have the power to appear in various forms such as animal, human or half human/animal shapes and could possess humans (MacMullen, *Christianizing the Roman Empire*, pp. 12-13).

readers as well as the average pagan, severely damaging the prospects of gaining the sympathy of public opinion. Among the masses it would have had the potential of frustrating Justin's whole protreptic purpose, even perhaps inciting calls for retribution against the Christians.

Justin's attack on polytheism was one that some pagans would have been willing to entertain, and Justin's citation of Socrates as an example of a noble pagan who died for the cause of monotheism would have stood him in good stead as Socrates still had many admirers. However, to equate all the gods of paganism with the evil demons (*1 Apol.* 9) would again have appeared overly simplistic, failing to recognise the predominant pagan belief that all daimons (whether good or bad) were inferior to and subject to the gods. If it were Justin's principal objective to convert his audience to Christianity, then an all-out onslaught against polytheism would have been appropriate. In the situation, though, where Justin's primary aim was to attain due process and toleration for the Christians it would have been more advantageous to avoid any attack that would have been regarded as a threat to the existing order, especially a politico-religious order that intricately involved the emperors themselves (for they were considered sons of Jupiter). It appears that in choosing to attack in this way Justin simply allowed his enthusiasm and passion for truth to get the better of him, revealing beliefs that should have remained in-house. Given the unity of religion and politics in the empire, the charge of disloyalty logically followed the charge of atheism. Justin's protreptic rhetoric pursued the only appropriate option: accentuate as much as possible Christian allegiance to the empire while highlighting the positive benefits flowing to it from Christian teachings and civic conduct. Justin's first salvo against the charge of disloyalty was to claim that there existed no conflict between a desire for the Kingdom of God and the empire (*1 Apol.* 11). Initially, such a claim appears innocuous, but did a desire for the Kingdom of God mean abandoning the empire? It was just as necessary to debunk the impression that Christians were only parasites living off the empire as it was to counter the notion that they were a cancerous element endangering more and more the empire's life. Thus, Justin declared that Christians "more than all other people" were "helpers and allies" in the promotion of peace and prosperity of the empire, for they practised virtue and shunned vice for fear of God's judgement and everlasting punishment (*1 Apol.* 12).

However, positive verbal declarations were insufficient. Justin needed to provide examples of vital practical support. What the empire desired above all else were peace and taxes. It appears that Justin was aware of this common cliché and was prepared to tell the government what would be pleasing to their ears. So we find him in the same chapter (*1 Apol.* 17) pledging Christian allegiance and prayers for the emperors, as well as an announcement that Christians pay all due taxes, all in accordance with the teachings of Christ. This also had value for reminding his Christian readers of their social obligations. On the other hand, Justin failed to mention that Christians were already participating in every aspect of Roman life, except the temples, a social fact increasing every decade.[93] Justin needed to produce hard evidence of this to prove that Christians were no longer simply "strangers and sojourners" but loyal dutiful citizens of the empire, thus giving weight to his implicit claim that the empire would be blessed if the Christians were given liberty of worship and allowed to prosper (*1 Apol.* 3).

The detail of Justin's description of Christian worship has been described as "remarkable in view of the fact that the *Apology* was primarily intended for a non-Christian public."[94] Its 'remarkableness' was certainly due to Justin's assessment of what

---

93 By the end of the second century AD Tertullian could boast that Christians were in the palace, senate, forum, and the military (*Apology* 42).
94 Barnard, *Justin Martyr*, p. 134.

he felt was necessary to counter the serious rumours of horrors allegedly perpetrated at Christian gatherings as a prerequisite for securing the desired change in judicial behaviour. The allegations of immorality being as detailed and pervasive as they were, it was only appropriate that Justin responded in depth with a thesis-cum-*suasoria*. At the same time Justin prudently endeavoured to keep his explanations simple, avoiding ecclesiastical terminology that would confuse or be unintelligible, for example, "Presider" (οπροεστώς) instead of bishop (επίσκοπος) in *1 Apol.* 65 and 67. Concerning the sacraments, however, Justin employed technical words such as "rebirth" and "eucharist" (*1 Apol.* 66) and presumed that, with explanation, these terms would be intelligible to a pagan audience.

As noted earlier, Justin introduced his explanation of Christian baptism and the eucharist "almost incidentally and without warning," undoubtedly in the hope of impressing his readers of the innocence of Christian rites. Concerning baptism, the Romans had some familiarity with similar practices as initiation rites existed in a number of the eastern mystery religions that had spread westwards across the empire. Justin's detailed description of Christian baptism was valuable for three reasons: firstly, it illustrated its external similarity to other forms of water baptism tolerated by the Romans, such as that performed in Mithraism; secondly, it showed that it was devoid of any offensive or crude elaborations found in other pagan rites, such as those practised in the initiation ritual of the popular cult of Cybele[95]; thirdly, it reminded Christian readers of the necessity and importance of the sacrament. Also, by emphasising that baptism was the beginning of a new life in which the recipient had to strive to

---

95 Converts to the Cybele cult were received via the *taurobolium*, or baptism of blood, in which they descended into a pit below a slaughtered ox, and after suffering drops of blood to fall on their faces, emerged cleansed of sin to live a life of regeneration. The genitals of the bull, representing his sacred fertility, were placed in a consecrated vessel and dedicated to the goddess: W. Durant, *Caesar and Christ: A History of Roman Civilisation and of Christianity from their beginnings to AD 325*, Simon and Schuster, New York, 1972, pp. 524-525.

be fruitful in the Spirit, Justin dissociated it from any notion of 'magical' regeneration.

Justin's awareness of the allegations of cannibalism should have made him circumspect in outlining Christian beliefs on the eucharist. According to Barnard[96], Justin "gives no real explanation or theory of the eucharist. He was content to accept its spiritual blessings without questioning how the elements had become the flesh and blood of Christ." However, in Colson's opinion Justin did at least employ analogy in *1 Apol.* 66 to explain his eucharistic thought[97]:

> To me it seems clear that the μεταβολή is merely the ordinary conversion of food into constituents of the human body which takes place whenever we eat, and that his point is that the change in the consecrated elements is analogous to this ... this everyday wonder makes the eucharistic miracle more credible ... [Justin could maintain] ... though some philosophical opinion has declared this to be impossible, our best scientific authorities have declared it to be a fact. Is it then an incredible thing that this should be repeated in another and higher sphere?

Hamilton[98] concurs with Colson, noting that Justin may well have been aware of Galen's physiological work, Περι Φυσικω'ν δυνάμεων (On Physical Forces), "which taught that the conversion of food is primarily into blood, the formation of flesh from blood being a secondary process." Hamilton concludes that Justin's use of such an analogy was "especially plausible" considering his pagan audience, "i.e., the use of analogies from

---

96 Barnard, *St. Justin Martyr*, p. 148.
97 F. H. Colson, "Notes and Studies," *Journal of Theological Studies* 23 (1922), pp. 161-171 at pp.167 and 168.
98 J. Hamilton, "Justin's *Apology*, 66. A Review of Scholarship and a Suggested Synthesis," *Ephemerides Theologicae Lovanienses* 48 (1979), pp. 554-560 at p. 558.

natural science involving pagan sources in order to present the plausibility of eucharistic change (aptitude of bread and wine for transformation into human blood)."[99]

However, even if Justin's analogy was apt to explain how bread and wine could change into flesh and blood, in exposing with such realism the whole doctrine of the eucharist to the full view of pagan readers Justin certainly pushed the boundaries of prudence. He makes no attempt to reinterpret the language of Christian worship in terms that might be more congenial to outsiders.[100] Was Justin's straightforwardness the product of calculated risk taking or simple-mindedness? Justin was gambling much if he believed that his description of the eucharistic food ("that the food eucharistised through the word of prayer that is from Him, from which our blood and flesh are nourished by transformation, is the flesh and blood of that Jesus who became incarnate": *1 Apol.* 66) would not have caused concern to uninitiated pagans. Certainly Christian catechumens would have benefited from such an exposition, but addressed to persons who had never attended a eucharistic celebration it would have only confirmed the criminal allegation of cannibalism in their minds. Nonetheless, what was the alternative for Justin? To explain the eucharist risked confirming the allegation of cannibalism; to remain silent would have left the same allegation unchallenged. Neither was an invitation to view a eucharistic celebration without any preceding detailed explanation a possibility for the same reasons mentioned earlier.

Justin's claim that Christian morality was not only consistent with the best of Graeco-Roman mores but provided a superior way of life was an audacious tactic both to comprehensively rebut and turn the tables on pagan accusations of immorality.

---

99 Hamilton, "Justin's *Apology*," p. 558.
100 R. L. Wilken, *The Spirit of Early Christian Thought*, Yale University Press, New Haven and London, 2003, pp. 30-31.

It amounted to a further *apodeixis* in support of Justin's demand for judicial justice. Of itself, it was not perilous for Justin to advance a new and superior ideal if he could simultaneously demonstrate that it would contribute to the betterment of the empire. The ancients were always willing to acknowledge fresh and lofty principles even if they themselves were not keen to practise them. At the same time, Christian readers would have been fortified in their moral convictions and encouraged to continue living the life of exceptional virtue.

Two conditions needed to be satisfied, however, if Justin's 'superiority' rhetoric was to be effective. First, it was necessary to present the higher standard always reaffirming the agreed basic standard, avoiding any form of 'one-upmanship' that would have offended the Romans as arrogant. This Justin mostly satisfied, boasting only on one occasion of the many examples of sexually pure Christians (*1 Apol.* 15). He did, though, tread on dangerous ground when he indicted the deification of Antinous, the young male lover of the emperor Hadrian (*1 Apol.* 29), in order to make the point that even the emperors were not immune from sexual vices. Many among the general Roman public might have considered Hadrian's action to be ridiculous; however, it was certainly not politic to include such an indictment in a formal petition addressed to Antoninus, Hadrian's adopted son. Justin was on safer ground when he adopted the language of Stoic-Cynic morality to target those popular vices considered reprehensible to the noble and aristocratic philosophical mind (such as fornication, homosexuality, adultery, divorce, incest, abortion and infant exposure). It was not unreasonable for Justin to do this, as pagan writers themselves before him had done the same, and would have gained the sympathy of those in authority who shared the same concerns. Likewise, it was certainly wise to attribute the higher morality to their root cause, namely, the Christian God, for as alluded to earlier, philosophers believed that right living came from right belief.

The second condition for the success of Justin's superiority rhetoric was the need to substantiate that the higher principles of Christians were not anti-social, such as the extreme encratic principles of heretics such as Tatian and Marcion, who both opposed marriage for all Christians. To the outsider, there would have appeared very little difference between the position of the heretics and Justin's rhetoric when advancing the Christian practices of virginity and continence. Galen recognised Christian virginity as in accord with the practice of genuine philosophers but Justin showed that it was a lifestyle lived by Christian people of ordinary stock, mostly uneducated people who dedicated their lives to God (*1 Apol.* 15). Though not a positively injurious practice there still needed to be care in presenting Christian sexual asceticism as in harmony with the continuation of the Graeco-Roman social structure through marriage and procreation. This he did in two ways: first, by defending the sanctity of marriage and procreation against divorce, contraception and abortion Justin showed Christian conformity to the general duty of maintaining the social order (as well as pre-empting the influence among mainstream Christians of heretics such as Tatian and Marcion); second, by quoting the words of Christ, "but all cannot receive this saying" (Matt. 19:11). So while praising virginity as a virtue Justin presented it as the exception, not the norm. It was simply a difference between the "good" (marriage) and the "better" (virginity).

Where there were profound differences in other areas of morality between Christianity and paganism, such as remarriage after divorce, Justin would have needed to defend the higher Christian standard against the accusation of unreasonableness. Most pagans would have considered the Christian total prohibition of divorce as unreasonable, even though pagan culture did not view divorce as something good in itself. The same would have been the case for the prohibition of lustful glances and impure thoughts of the heart. Though most pagans would have dismissed such teachings as impossible extremes, they would certainly have struck a cord of sympathy with the Stoic ideal of disciplining the instincts in pursuit of rational goals. Justin did not directly address the question of reasonableness in *1 Apol.* 15 but did state earlier that innocent differences should not be grounds for outlawing or persecuting Christianity (*1 Apol.* 8); and, despite their loftiness, the higher ethical principles of Christianity would bring about a morally improved society—a goal in accord with the desires of the Stoic emperors.

The Argument from Beliefs

Purpose: To establish Christian innocence against the charges of atheism, immorality and disloyalty

There was no tendency in Justin to mitigate or water down traditional Christian beliefs in the face of pagan sensibilities, including beliefs about God, creation, the incarnation, the bloodshed of the cross, the Church, the resurrection of the flesh and the Last Things.[101] Concerning God, Justin was the first Christian to respond in writing to the charge of atheism,[102] making the paradoxical confession that "we are atheists with reference to gods such as these, but not with reference to the

---

101 Chadwick, *Early Christian Thought*, p. 19. Chadwick makes the observation that "[a]lthough he [Justin] never sets out to give a single, succinct statement of his beliefs, it is possible to piece together a mosaic providing a clear and surprisingly full account of his doctrines ... "

102 D. W. Palmer, "Atheism, Apologetic, and Negative Theology in the Greek Apologists of the Second Century," *Vigiliae Christianae* 37 (1983), pp. 234-259 at p. 241.

most true God" (*1 Apol.* 6). The Christian God was "the Father of righteousness and temperance … who is unmixed with evil" (*1 Apol.* 6). This God was not the innovation of Christians, but the God who revealed himself to Moses in earlier times (*1 Apol.* 62), the creator of all things (*1 Apol.* 10).[103] Despite knowing that some derided as madness the Christian belief of Jesus' divinity, Justin unhesitantly declared "the first power after God the Father and Master of all is the Word, who is also Son; and of Him, in what follows, we will tell how He took flesh and became man" (*1 Apol.* 32). God was the Father of the Son, begotten for the purpose of fully revealing the true God and dying on the cross so that the sins of humanity could be forgiven and that "the bodies of men and women … [should] rise again in God's appointed time and put on incorruption. … for … 'the things that are impossible with men are possible with God'" (*1 Apol.* 19).

Appropriateness of the argument

As part of his protreptic endeavour to secure a change in judicial policy towards the Christians, it was both inevitable and necessary that Justin provide some form of detailed exposition of Christian beliefs to bolster his claims of innocence. The authorities would have expected such a forensic outline to determine whether the picture of Christian behaviour painted by Justin was more than just an ideal portrayal or sham facade. Likewise, philosophers believing that behaviour followed from belief would have expected an outline of beliefs to test Justin's claim that both Christian behaviour and its theoretical basis were worthy of the term 'philosophy.' Christians, particularly

---

103 Justin is here also concerned to attack the heresy of Marcion. God is the creator of all things out of love, and created the universe for man's sake. See Osborn, *Justin Martyr*, pp. 45 and 51.

neophytes, would have benefited through having a valuable catechetical resource at hand.

Providing an exposition of beliefs also laid the foundation for one of Justin's more important arguments, similitude, the significance of which will be discussed and assessed later. Even where Justin's exposition highlighted significant differences between Christian and pagan beliefs it showed that Christian beliefs were nevertheless harmless to both individuals and the empire as a whole.

However, whether they were harmful or not, there was still risk of Justin causing offence in revealing particular Christian beliefs to his imperial audience. Hence, the need for Justin to couch his language in terms agreeable to them. Space prohibits an examination of each in detail; nevertheless, one example is belief in the resurrection in the flesh. This belief was undoubtedly startling and distasteful, contrary to what normally passed for wisdom among the educated. A case could be made that discussion of this and other doctrines should have been excluded from *1 Apology* to avoid unnecessary controversies as well as to reduce its prolixity. Then again, this would have been difficult for Justin, who firmly believed in the objective reasonableness of all Christian beliefs and optimistically assumed that full and frank explanations were the best means to win over the sincere and open-minded.

It was a different matter, though, with respect to Christian beliefs about God. It was absolutely necessary for Justin to outline Christian theism to rebut the charges of atheism, and such an outline couched in the language of monotheism would have been respected by philosophically-minded Romans and Greeks already attracted to the concept.

The Argument from Due Process

Purpose: To end arbitrary injustice committed by the state

In the opening chapters of *1 Apology* Justin's rhetoric appeals to the emperors' sense of reason and justice as pious philosophers[104] seeking an end to the naked injustice of condemning Christians simply for their name without any evidence of crimes committed by them except for "evil rumour":

> ... if nobody can prove anything against us, true reason forbids you, because of an evil rumour, to wrong innocent people ... the rulers should give their decision as having followed, not violence and tyranny, but piety and philosophy ... (*1 Apol.* 3).

According to Justin, if the emperors were sincere seekers of truth then it followed without question that they "should honour and love only the truth."[105] This could occur only if the emperors judged the charges against Christians "after an exact and searching enquiry, not moved by prejudice ... nor irrational impulse or long prevalent rumours" (*1 Apol.* 2).

If proper inquiry were made it would find that the Christian name was in fact χρηστός (Chrestos), that is, excellent (*1 Apol.* 4).

However, if upon proper inquiry the charges against the Christians were in fact substantiated then the Christians deserved to be punished (*1 Apol.* 3). Otherwise, the emperors should not yield to "unreasoning passion" excited by the demons (*1 Apol.* 5) or the deceptions of evil spirits and "do nothing

---

104 In fact, the words "pious" and "philosopher" each appear four times in the first three chapters of *1 Apology*. (1.1; 2.1; 2.2; 3.2). Barnard, *St. Justin Martyr*, p. 15, sees in Justin's bold appeal for justice an imitation of Plato's *Apology*.

105 *1 Apol.* 2. Osborn, *Justin Martyr*, p. 79: "The Stoic devotion to truth was no less than that of Plato." Justin would have been hoping to see the emperors apply the Stoic creed "*Amicus Plato, magis amica veritas*" in favour of Christianity.

unreasonable" (*1 Apol.* 12). Justin added that such a "fair and righteous challenge" would reap benefit for both rulers and ruled (*1 Apol.* 3), but to ignore his request would only result in undermining the happiness of the state.[106]

Justin also noted that the Romans tolerated some of their own who denied and insulted the pagan gods, and that those same even received prizes and honours. It seemed grossly inconsistent to Justin that Christians who did likewise were singled out for persecution:

> And of these some taught atheism; and the poets who have flourished among you raise a laugh out of the uncleanness of Jupiter with his own children. And those who now adopt such instruction are not restrained by you; but, on the contrary, you bestow prizes and honours upon those who euphoniously insult the gods (*1 Apol.* 4).

Moreover, in *2 Apology*, Justin considered it shameful that those who charged Christians with immorality were guilty of the same:

> Be ashamed, be ashamed, you who charge the guiltless with those deeds which you yourselves openly commit, and who ascribe things which refer to yourselves and to your gods to those who have no part in them. Be you converted; become wise (*2 Apol.* 12).[107]

Justin employed strong epideictic rhetoric in this sentence. He

---

106 In *1 Apol.* 3 Justin paraphrases a remark made by Socrates and found in the fifth book of Plato's *Republic*: "For even one of the ancients somewhere said, 'Unless both rulers and ruled philosophise, it is impossible to make states blessed.'" Cf. M. O. Young, "Justin, Socrates and the Middle-Platonists," *Studia Patristica* 18/2 (1989), pp. 161-165 at p. 162.

107 Justin also remarked in *2 Apology* that his writings were not as injurious to public morality as other works by the Sotadists, Philaenidians, Dancers, and Epicureans that were authorised by the Romans (*2 Apol.* 15).

did not address or try to prove Christian innocence in the face of allegations of immorality, but attempted to turn the tables to expose his accusers of hypocrisy and double standards.

Furthermore, Justin argued that religious tolerance should be extended to the Christians even though the Romans disagreed with their beliefs, for their beliefs were of no threat to other individuals or Roman society as a whole:

> And if anyone says that this [Christian teaching] is incredible or impossible, this mistake of ours is one which concerns us only, and no one else, as long as we are not convicted of doing any evil (*1 Apol.* 8).

Justin's request for a change in judicial behaviour was only part of a larger protreptic endeavour. A change of behaviour was necessary before any change of belief system. For Justin, it was a three-step progression: cease persecuting Christians simply for their name; afford them due process when tried so that their innocence may be manifested in the face of the charges of atheism, immorality and disloyalty; and in the process the truth of their beliefs would become self-evident to any philosopher worthy of the name. A legal precedent providing the desired due process free from violent attacks and mob accusation apparently existed in the rescript of Hadrian, and was cited by Justin at the end of *1 Apology* (*1 Apol.* 68).

Appropriateness of the argument

Justin's appeal for justice and due process was *prima facie* reasonable and appropriate considering Roman legal principles and procedures. Justin's protreptic tactic was to play on the emperors' reputation for piety and justice to move them to ensure that Christians were judged according to these formal principles, etc. There was no attempt to seek escape from inquiry or justice; Justin admitted that Christians actually guilty of crimes or immorality should be punished without fear or favour. His was therefore an appeal based firmly on objective legal principle: namely, irrespective of all else, every individual should be afforded due process and not merely condemned out of hand and should be tried in overt and impartial proceedings solely on the basis of moral character and conduct, free from hypocrisy and double standards. This all amounted not to an overthrow of the Roman legal system but its enforcement in line with its own high principles.

Justin's use of the word *Chrestos* was rhetorical *ethos* to erect the moral authority of the Christian name. Often the Christian name was wrongly spelt χρηστός and Christians were described as χρηστιανοί. *Chrestos* was both an adjective and a proper name, whereas *Christos* meant nothing to most people. The difference in pronunciation would have been minor, and Justin took advantage of such for his protreptic objectives. If it was wrong to condemn someone simply for his or her name, it was doubly wrong when that name was excellent. Yet, that was just what Roman justice was guilty of.

However, Justin's argument for due process and toleration would have been considered seriously flawed by the Roman authorities for one significant reason: the Roman government placed no obstacle against the freedom and dissemination of new or foreign religions on the condition that *they participated in the official imperial cult.* This cult, begun during the reign of Domitian and assiduously promoted by the Antonines, involved according divine honours to the 'genius' of the living emperor and belief in his deification after death.[108] Nonetheless, to do such was impossible for any Christian without committing formal apostasy. Any refusal by Christians to accord such honours to the emperor *ipso facto* placed them in conflict with

---

108 The imperial cult was "the public association of emperors with gods, divine forces, sacred rites, altars and temples … During the Antonine age, this imperial gospel saw its culmination with the representations of the emperors as the divinely elected viceregent of Jupiter on earth": Rhee, *Early Christian Literature*, pp. 160 and 162.

the established Roman order and, further, was considered an impiety that endangered the *pax deorum*, or goodwill of the gods on which the prosperity of the empire depended. Therefore, how was it possible for the Romans to grant religious liberty to what was for them a new and atheistic superstition that denied worship according to the tradition of the fathers and desired to substitute what was best in *Romanitas*, namely reason, virtue and love of fatherland, with an insanity (*morbis mentis*) that was by its very nature a social revolution? Christians not only deserved ostracism, but also punishment for their 'evil.' Considering that Justin singled out "atheism" as the most serious slander against Christians both with regard to the political and legal consequences that followed (*1 Apol.* 6; *2 Apol.* 3), he should have included in his petition a *modus vivendi* with the Roman authorities regarding emperor worship, something the Romans would have considered essential in any application for toleration.

Such a *modus vivendi* would have drawn a distinction between worship of the emperor and the political allegiance due to him. Justin could have stressed that Christians were willing to live as loyal citizens under emperors whose power was certainly of divine origin (as taught in Christian Scripture: John 19:11; Rom. 13:1-6), but that divinity was the Christian God rather than Jupiter, something implied in *1 Apol.* 17 ("every person will suffer punishment in eternal fire according to the merit of his actions, and will give account according to the ability he has received from God"). However, any such proposal would have secularised the imperial person, something inconceivable to the second-century Roman mind. Coming also from a representative of a "third race" that was still numerically and socially insignificant[109] such a secularisation was politically still centuries away from being achievable, and so for Justin's

---

109 According to Rhee, *Early Christian Literature*, p. 10, Christianity in AD 150 had only 40,000 adherents (or 0.07 percent of the empire's population).

generation a forlorn impossibility.

In mentioning the pernicious influence of the demons Justin attempted to set a 'literary trap' for the emperors, relying on their reputation for piety (that is, in the Roman sense of respect for the 'true gods'), as opposed to superstition[110] and magic. Justin's rhetoric had the potential to equate the emperors and Christians as both opposed to superstition and magic. That being the case, the former could not reasonably condemn the latter. Whether or not Justin believed the emperors' reputation for piety to be justified, he exploited it to warn that they should not become dupes of creatures who promoted injustice and impiety and who persecuted the followers of reason throughout history. The demon's hatred of reason made them natural enemies of the pious emperors also; and the emperors should be made to recognise this and yield respect to the Christians as partners in the same struggle and as successors to the heroic philosophers.

Justin pointed the literary finger at the demons in order to diminish the impression that he was directly attacking the emperors for their legal plight. However, Justin made precarious statements that either directly accused the emperors or left ambiguous the extent to which they were subject to demonic influence and morally accountable for their bondage. For example, in *1 Apol.* 5 Justin actually accused the emperors of "giving in to unreasoning passion, and the instigation of evil demons," while in *2 Apol.* 1 he expressly charged that the Prefect Urbicus was incited by and even served the demons in his condemnation of Christians. It thus appeared that Justin was engaging in an outright indictment of Roman imperial

---

110 The term 'superstition' in the educated Roman or Greek sense was used to designate religious groups or practices alien to the Roman virtues of piety, justice, philanthropy, etc.: Wilken, "Toward a Social Interpretation of Early Christian Apologetics," pp. 438 and 447.

power as a form of demonic tyranny and that the emperors themselves and their underlings were no more than puppets. Such an attack would have reinforced the sense of injustice and need for change among his Christian readers. However, by it Justin exceeded the boundaries of the ancient prerogative of *parrhēsia*, or right of philosophers to frankly instruct and reprove rulers and it was inconsistent with comments he made elsewhere recognising and respecting the political authority of the emperors and praying for them (*1 Apol.* 17).

First impressions count and if any of the authorities read Justin's words in *1 Apol.* 5 or *2 Apol.* 1 they would have summarily dismissed Justin's demands on the grounds that his language was inconceivably insolent and insulting, if not treasonable. At the same time, any hope of making a favourable presentation of Christianity for the purpose of converting anyone in government would have been irretrievably lost. It would not have been enough for Justin to argue that he was attempting to prove the loyalty of Christians by warning the authorities about the truth of evil plots and disguises. Simply to suggest that the demons instigated the judicial enforcement of imperial laws against the Christians was insult enough; and if these laws themselves were inspired by the demons and on that account ought not to be obeyed, therein lay the treason.

Assuming its authenticity and inclusion by Justin, Hadrian's rescript appeared to offer a relatively quick and easy means to convince public opinion that Christians should be afforded due process. If Justin's interpretation of it was correct then there existed an imperial precedent insisting that Christians be only condemned if they "broke the law." Nonetheless, Justin subsequently discounted the rescript, restating that his demand for due process for the Christians was fair in itself, irrespective of whether any imperial legislation purporting to give them relief existed or not (*1 Apol.* 68). However, Justin's reference to the rescript still had the benefit of providing an example of Christian acknowledgement of Roman imperial authority and law (albeit out of self-interest) at a time when Christians were being accused of possessing no respect for either.

The Argument from Threat

Purpose: To end arbitrary injustice committed by the state

Justin commenced *1 Apology* by employing epideictic rhetoric to idealise the emperors as "pious and philosophers and guardians of justice and lovers of culture" (*1 Apol.* 2). Later, Justin declared, "we worship God only, but in other things we gladly serve you … and praying that with your imperial power you may also be found to possess sound judgement" (*1 Apol.* 17).

However, in other places Justin spoke in a different tone, openly warning the emperors not to act unjustly lest they themselves incurred punishment for being iniquitous:

> For if, having learned the truth, you fail to do what is righteous, you have no defence before God (*1 Apol.* 3).

> … on the other hand, if we are found to have committed no wrong, either in the appellation of the name, or in our citizenship, you must be exceedingly anxious against incurring righteous judgement, by unjustly punishing those who are not convicted (*1 Apol.* 4).

The punishment with which Justin threatened the emperors was not of a temporal kind but "the eternal punishment by fire" (*1 Apol.* 12, 18, 45).

Justin not only warned the emperors to act justly but also proceeded to compare their judicial abilities unfavourably to those of Christ's (*1 Apol.* 12). He even sarcastically questioned whether they sincerely desired their citizens to be law-abiding stating, "But you seem to fear lest all people become righteous, and you no longer have any to punish" (*1 Apol.* 12).

In this argument Justin simultaneously employed two forms of rhetorical proofs to achieve his protreptic purpose: *ethos* and *pathos*. Through *ethos*, he erected the God of the Christians as the ultimate judge and authority to which even the divine emperors must account; by *pathos* he intended to instil fear of eternal punishment if judicial justice was not granted to the Christians. Ultimately, these proofs combined into one argument of self-interest: that the emperors afford the Christians due process for their own sakes. It was a stark warning he repeated at the end of *1 Apology:*

> For we forewarn you, that you will not escape the coming judgement of God, if you continue unjust; and we ourselves cry out, "What is pleasing to God, let that be done" (*1 Apol.* 68).

Appropriateness of the argument

It was only appropriate for Justin in *1 Apol.* 2 to begin by employing epideictic rhetoric to sing the praises of the emperors as "guardians of justice and lovers of culture," praying also in *1 Apol.* 17 that they "possess sound judgement" in the exercise of their power. This was the wisest approach considering the delicate position of Christians. Demanding justice was Justin's prime reason for writing but it had to be done in language that clearly expressed respect and support for the emperors, while disavowing any form of political insubordination, treason or subversion of the empire.

Parrhēsia, or the freedom to offer words of advice or even forthright rebuke of rulers, was a prerogative traditionally accorded to philosophers since the classical age of Athens and continued well after Justin's martyrdom. Presenting his petition as one written by a philosopher, Justin obviously sought to exploit this privilege for his own protreptic purposes, employing a tactic common to rhetoricians. However, did Justin remain within the parameters of this privilege with his repeated threats of judgement and hell-fire directed at the emperors? Certainly other philosophers and poets spoke of the afterlife and punishments for the impious and unbelieving and Tertullian would later write that philosophers "with every kind of bitter speech ... flaunt[ed] their freedom unpunished even against the very emperors."[111] However, it must be remembered that Justin did not come from any established and respected philosophical tradition but was a member of an outlawed community believed to be nurturing subversive ideas. In no way, therefore, would Justin have enjoyed the same scope of freedom usually afforded to pagan philosophers to speak frankly to the emperors, and so by issuing threats of divine retribution he over-stepped the boundaries of what would have been considered a respectful petition or apology presented by a Christian. Justin should have limited himself to referring to injustices without implicating the emperors as personally responsible and liable to judgement. Acting as he did Justin changed his status from appellant to one of accuser and judge.

Nevertheless, whether respectful or not, the rhetorical worth of Justin's hell-fire threat from the standpoint of *ethos* is questionable. Why would any pagan reader(s) fear threats issued by a member of an outlawed novel religion in the name of a God they did not even recognise? Nor was the issuing of hell-fire threats a weapon only Christians could use. As Celsus[112] notes:

> just as you believe in eternal punishments, so also the interpreters of the mysteries, the priests and

---

111 Tertullian, *Ad Nationes* 1.4.
112 Origen, *Contra Celsum*, 8.48.

initiators, do the same. You threaten others with these punishments while they threaten you. It is possible to consider which of the two is nearer the truth or more successful.

For Celsus, and undoubtedly other pagan philosophers before and after him, no form of threat could stand alone as a viable argument; such needed to be supported by miracles, prophecies and other forms of divination.

In addition to his threats, Justin further undermined his own cause by his general contumacious tone of language when complaining about the injustices endured by Christians. The opening words of *2 Apology* provide a prime example of a rebuke that would have been perceived by any loyal Roman as inconceivably insolent:

> O Romans, what has recently happened in your city under Urbicus, and what is likewise being everywhere by the governors unreasonably, have compelled me to compose these arguments for your sakes, who are of like passion and are our brothers, *though you are ignorant of the fact and repudiate it on account of the splendour of your position (2 Apol.* 1).

All petitions addressed to the emperors had to be in obsequious and appealing language, regardless of the stature, power or wealth of the applicant. One expects that the obligation to be obsequious would have been even greater where the applicant was a member of a despised community. However, civility was certainly not a strong point in Justin's *Apologies*, a serious omission in writings addressed to emperors who possessed absolute power, claimed divine title, and required all subjects to eulogise suitably their justice and generosity when submitting petitions.

Nevertheless, a case could still be made that Justin's use of threat and tone of language served some valuable 'in-house' purposes. Such would have reinforced in his Christian readers the supremacy of the Christian God and his Christ over the so-called 'divine emperors,' providing hope that those responsible for the injustices would one day face retribution and the Christian peoples achieve vindication. In challenging both the titles and actions of the emperors Justin not only emulated his favourite philosopher Socrates but also prefigured to his readers the future pronouncement of Christ's judgement upon the persecutors. However, it is arguable that 'in-house' benefits of this kind could have been achieved by any number of other means, thus rendering it both unnecessary and imprudent on Justin's part to include threats and contumacious language in a public petition that risked provoking both summary rejection and hostility from the authorities.

The Argument from Similitude

Purpose: To show forth Christianity's rationality

In the words of Kennedy[113], early Christian apologetical literature "makes use of Greek philosophy and rhetoric in hopes of persuading those in positions of power to take a more sympathetic view of the Christians and especially to cease legal persecution of them." Upon his conversion to the "only safe and useful philosophy" (*Dial.* 8) Justin became aware that Christianity and pagan philosophy shared similar beliefs in a number of important areas. Reflecting on these truths as found in pagan philosophy Justin sought to recognise them as a *praeparatio evangelica*, a preparation for the gospel, planted by the work of the *Logos*-Christ.[114] In so doing, Justin has been

---

113 Kennedy, *Classical Rhetoric*, 133.
114 C. Schönborn, "Does the Church Need Philosophy?," *Communio* 15 (1988), pp. 334-349 at p. 343.

regarded as a precursor of Christian humanism and a model of those Christians who seek the conversion of the noble and intellectual pagan.

Justin also sought to take advantage of these similarities to construct another argument in support of his protreptic demands for a change in judicial behaviour. By virtue of his own journey through philosophy (*Dial.* 2) Justin had first-hand experience of how the pagan philosophical schools not only offered their own systems of metaphysics but also proposed moral ideals and religious ways of life. Justin was therefore well qualified to construct an *apodeixis* highlighting the significant instances of "common ground" between Christianity and philosophical paganism.[115] Through establishing similitude Justin hoped to elevate the status of Christianity in the eyes of educated opponents and thereby circumvent the fear and hostility which denied it the intellectual and legal freedom enjoyed by other philosophies: "Receive us, even if you receive us only on an equality with them [Empedocles, Pythagoras, Plato, Socrates and Homer], who believe in God not less but more firmly than they do" (*1 Apol.* 18).

The identifiable similarities between Christianity and paganism can be divided into two categories: (i) 'external' similarities and (ii) 'internal' similarities. With regard to the first, Justin witnessed how the various philosophical schools actively competed with each other for converts and those who underwent a 'philosophical conversion' adopted both cognitive and behavioural changes so as to imitate their new philosophical exemplars. In the competition between schools there were preachers and missionaries who

---

115 According to Droge, "Restoration of Philosophy," p. 306, the writers Justin principally had in mind were the Stoics, and above all the Platonists. Barnard, *St. Justin Martyr*, p. 58, notes, "In the two *Apologies* there are nine classical quotations—six from Plato, two from Xenophon and one from Euripides."

delivered public speeches recommending their philosophy as the unique way to truth and happiness while exposing the flaws of the alternatives. Such competition was engaged in all the major cities of the empire. Christianity as a school of philosophy acted no differently and Justin sought to impress this point through the wearing of philosophical garb when proselytising (*Dial.* 1). In such circumstances, where was the consistency or justice in persecuting Christianity if its external promotional activities were always peaceful and consistent with all the respected philosophical schools of the day?

Establishing similarity in belief possessed an even greater potential to reduce the alien status of Christianity and its level of inferiority compared with the established wisdom. If the Christian had knowledge and respect for Homer, Plato and Socrates then he ought to be given a respectful hearing as a fellow philosopher—and perhaps 'Christ the philosopher' had something worth pronouncing after all. Justin could point to a number of shared beliefs with Plato and the Stoics, including creation, periodical catastrophes (the last being Noah's flood, known as the flood of *Deucalion* to the Stoics: *2 Apol.* 7), the end of the world, and punishment after death (*1 Apol.* 8).

Furthermore, Christian beliefs regarding Jesus of Nazareth as the only-begotten Son of God, who was crucified, resurrected and ascended into heaven, were no more reprehensible or incredible than the opinions of authors such as Homer, Empedocles, Pythagoras, Plato or Socrates (*1 Apol.* 18) or what was believed of pagan deities such as Jupiter, Mercury, Asclepius, Perseus or Bacchus (*1 Apol.* 21, 22). In addition, the Christian God was identifiable with the God of Socrates and the later Middle Platonists; that is, the One who was inscrutable, transcendent, immutable, nameless, unmoved first cause, unutterable, unbegotten, without parts or passions (*1 Apol.* 9, 10, 13, 25, 49, 53, 61, 63; *2 Apol.* 6, 12). Finally, the Christian rejection of idolatry resembled that found in the writings of Socrates and the poet Menander:

> … and while we maintain that people ought not to worship the works of their hands, we say the very things which have been said by the comic poet Menander, and others who have said this, for they have declared that the Demiurge is greater than the things formed (*1 Apol.* 20).

> And Socrates, who was more forcible in this direction than all of them, was accused of the very same crimes as ourselves. For they said that he was introducing new divinities, and did not consider those to be gods whom the state recognised (*2 Apol.* 10).[116]

By pursuing similitude Justin ultimately aimed to render the singling out of Christianity for persecution unjustifiable (*1 Apol.* 24). However, Justin saw only limited value in this argument. It could only take him so far. Truth was more important than similarity (*1 Apol.* 23); Jesus was superior to the sons of Zeus (*1 Apol.* 22). Christianity was no ordinary philosophy, it was the only safe and useful philosophy, preserved in the writings of the prophets, possessing a teaching "more complete and worthy of God" (*1 Apol.* 20). Adherents of this true philosophy were not unlike the much-revered Socrates,[117] who contested an identical philosophical struggle against the demons for the sake of reason and truth, only to be persecuted, just as Christians were persecuted for the name of Christ.

---

116 Justin is quoting Xenophon, among others, who recorded that Socrates was convicted for "refusing to recognise the gods the city recognises and introducing new divinities" (*Memorabilia* 1.1.1).

117 In the philosophical milieu of the age "there was a deep reverence for the philosopher martyred to death, the great model of course being Socrates" according to Skarsaune, "The Conversion of Justin Martyr," p. 66. Osborn, *Justin Martyr*, p. 82, states that Justin "is the first Christian writer to link the name of Socrates with that of Christ … In fact, the only ante-Nicene Greek fathers who speak ill of Socrates are Theophilus of Antioch and the writer of the Clementine Homilies."

Appropriateness of the argument

Justin's highlighting of similarities between Christianity and pagan philosophy and writers was deliberately calculated knowing that the emperors were also Stoic philosophers who admired and generously supported such men of wisdom, both Latin and Greek. It was unquestionably the most judicious course of action to take to raise the intellectual profile of the Christians and dispose Justin's pagan addressees to hear his petition with some amount of patience and respect. Furthermore, there was no inherent danger in giving only qualified support for the existing philosophies of the day, as it was normal practice for men of wisdom to engage in intellectual criticism of rival philosophies.

Justin's use of similitude had particular potential for effectiveness with regards to 'difficult' Christian beliefs, including the virgin birth, the divinity of Christ and the resurrection. Such beliefs were not only difficult but in some cases impossible according to pagan rationale. Also, claims about the end of the age and a coming kingdom were unverifiable hypotheses that could not be tested according to the rigorous standards of philosophers and rhetors. The latter considered that belief in such things was uncritical acceptance of nonsense. To highlight, therefore, that pagans already ascribed to beliefs that were analogous to these amounted to a persuasive revelation, breaking down objections and blunting ridicule.

Justin's employment of philosophical categories and concepts to illustrate the harmony between Christian and pagan philosophical monotheism was the high point in his similitude argument and demonstrated Christianity's growing philosophical competence. Since both Christians and certain pagans acknowledged that there was only one God ("Father and maker of the universe"[118]), it was patently absurd that Christians alone should be singled out and persecuted as atheists. No philosopher of the school of Middle Platonism

---

118 This phrase comes from Plato's *Timaeus* 28c (ποιητης και πατηρ του' παντός).

who employed the language of negative theology to describe the one God was so treated, therefore Justin reasoned neither should Christians who appropriated identical terms. The same applied for Christianity's attack on popular polytheism as it mirrored the Academy's established philosophical critique. There remained only the practical difficulty of presenting other difficult doctrines and teachings of Christianity in appropriate philosophical terms to enable intellectual pagans with their own cultural backgrounds and circumstances to identify with them.

Another example of similitude was in regards to martyrdom. Christians were mocked for dying for their beliefs (*2 Apol.* 4). Marcus Aurelius himself would write later that Christian martyrdom was mere stubbornness for an illusion.[119] Yet the concept of suffering and contempt for physical pain for the sake of truth and honour existed in Graeco-Roman funerary orations, philosophical discourses, novels and biographies. Voluntary death for principle in defiance of tyranny (for example, Socrates as the "philosopher-martyr") as noted earlier was recognised and honoured by the great Stoics. The Roman tradition of the military sacramentum venerated heroic self-destruction as a means of redeeming one's lost honour.

To show that Christianity engaged in only peaceful proselytism similar to the philosophical schools had the advantage of discounting fear of the messenger, thus enabling Justin to present his Christ not as a malevolent destroyer of the Graeco-Roman philosophical tradition but as one peacefully supplementing and correcting the wisdom of the ancients. This was important for since the burning of Rome in AD 64 Christians were somewhat stigmatised as anti-social and seeking the destruction of the Roman order.[120] Justin's highlighting of shared beliefs

---

119 Aurelius, *Meditations* 3.16; 11.3.

120 The problem was compounded by certain Christian groups outside the Great Church, such as the New Prophecy movement of Montanus based in Phrygia in Asia Minor, who lived in relative communal isolation waiting and hoping for the apocalyptic to occur. The Romans either could not or did not necessarily care to distinguish between mainstream and 'heretical' Christians.

in periodic catastrophes was also of critical importance here. It was necessary for him to show that, while mainstream Christians did believe in the apocalyptic, these beliefs were no more threatening than those held by contemporary Platonists and Stoics and that Christians were not in such radical enmity with the empire that they subversively desired its destruction.

The Argument from Dependence (Source)

Purpose: To recommend Christianity as the only safe and useful philosophy

In Justin's mind, not only did Christianity and pagan philosophy or cult share certain similarities, they shared these similarities for two important reasons:

(i) Philosophers had borrowed teachings from the prophets.

(ii) The work of Christ who, as the pre-existent and eternal *Logos*, continually planted seeds of truth among all peoples and philosophies throughout all ages.[121]

---

121 It may seem that Justin was attempting to "hedge his bets," that is, claiming that similitude in philosophy/cult was due either to demonic imitation or dependence on respectable sources. What criterion was employed by Justin to determine the source of a notable similarity, at least in regards to philosophy? Chadwick, *Early Christian Thought*, p. 13, offers one suggestion as a starting point: "… the *higher philosophical truths about God* were not acquired by pagan philosophers through any diabolical agency. They came from wholly respectable sources: either by derivation from the writings of Moses or through the exercise of the divinely given reason" (italics added). However, what of *all other philosophical truths* held by pagans? Should their derivation be automatically ascribed to demonic influence? Justin certainly does not argue this. As shall be seen when treating his doctrine on the *Logos*, it is primarily through the influence of the *Logos* planting 'seeds of truth' in all minds that pagan writers acquired these residual philosophical truths, enabling them to rightly exercise their divinely given reason.

The first reason, otherwise known as the "loan" theory, lists elements in the philosophical tradition that supposedly were derived from the Scriptures written by Moses and then calls attention to Moses' chronological priority over the Greek philosophers. Justin expressed his form of the argument as follows:

> And everything both philosophers and poets have said concerning the immortality of the soul, or punishments after death, or contemplation of heavenly things, or doctrines like these, they have received such hints from the prophets as have enabled them to understand and expound these things (*1 Apol.* 44).

Through the argument of dependence Justin could simultaneously accomplish two things in support of his protreptic objectives: (i) establish similitude with paganism; and (ii) establish the superiority of Christianity. As evidence of dependence Justin repeatedly cited Plato as an example of one who borrowed extensively from Moses. In his view, Plato relied on Moses in the following instances: to prove the freedom of the human will (*1 Apol.* 44); for his account of the origin of the world (*1 Apol.* 59); and in his references to Second and Third Powers "next to the first God" (*1 Apol.* 60).[122]

When highlighting similitude, Plato was for Justin the intellectual bridge leading to the better, 'more ancient philosophers.' Arguing dependence, Plato was portrayed as reliant on the ancients, that is, the Old Testament prophets. In this way, Justin equated the esteemed philosopher with himself (and Christians in general) and Plato became a forerunner and

---

122 Though Moses was unaware of any doctrine of the Trinity as such, Justin believed that his account of the brazen serpent on the figure of a cross in the book of Numbers and his mention of "the Spirit of God mov(ing) over the waters" in Genesis were the sources of Plato's discussion of other "Powers" … "next to the first God."

an ally rather than a leader.

Justin also turned his attention to the Stoics and declared:

> And hear how the prophetic Spirit signified through
> Moses that there would be a conflagration. He spoke
> thus: 'Everliving fire will descend and will devour
> even to the abyss below.' It is not, then, that we hold
> the same opinions as others, but that all speak in
> imitation of ours (*1 Apol.* 60).

However, despite dependence the philosophers still fell into errors and contradictions:

> And hence there seem to be seeds of truth among all
> people; but they are proved not to have understood
> them accurately when they contradict each other (*1
> Apol.* 44).

Justin wished to advance dependence on the prophets in addition to the argument of similitude to show that true wisdom and philosophy were actually found in Scripture, which now belonged to the Christians, and that any truth possessed by paganism came only through borrowing from the older literature of the Hebrews. The pagans took wisdom from the storehouse of Moses but corrupted it, only for Christianity to finally come and both restore divine truth and bring it to perfection. Knowledge of such dependence should not only provoke an end to the injustices committed against Christians but also inspire the adoption of Christianity as the primary source of perfect truth.

Justin's argument of dependence based on the work of Christ as the pre-existent and eternal *Logos* was developed to counter the following accusation: if the God of the Christians created the world, then why was Jesus of Nazareth not known and active from the beginning? In answer to this question Justin appropriated the philosophical concept of the *Logos Spermatikos* (σπερματικός λόγος) and moulded it to argue for Christ's ever-present work among humanity (and hence historical priority), to claim ownership of all truth wherever found, and to claim for Christianity the status of the unique bearer of all truth unsullied by error. Quasten[123] identifies Justin's concept of the *Logos* as his "most important doctrine ... because it forms a bridge between pagan philosophy and Christianity."

Justin interpreted the *Logos* as the "germinating word" that was active throughout history planting and inspiring seeds (σπέρματα) of truth in the reason of all men and women.[124] Again, Justin consequently had no difficulty acknowledging that within paganism there certainly existed truth, this time due to the work of the *Logos* among pagans:

> And those of the Stoic school, since they are honourable at least in their ethical teaching, as were also the poets in some particulars, on account of a seed of logos implanted in every race of men and women (*2 Apol.* 8).

The *Logos* acted among noteworthy pagan philosophers such as Socrates in order to condemn vice and idolatry, and such discernment was the great distinction of Greek philosophy.[125] In fact, all rational thought and right moral conduct was evidence of the universally active and present *Logos*. In this way, the *Logos* was the principle for natural revelation. However, because the ancients had only a partial and limited participation in the Logos this led to contradictions between the various pagan philosophies

---

123 Quasten, *Patrology*, vol. 1, p. 209. Chadwick, "Justin Martyr's Defence," p. 295, states, "the Logos theology is not just a piece of propagandist language to build a rickety bridge to his Platonic and Stoic friends. We find in the Dialogue that Justin cannot adequately expound his faith without philosophical help."

124 The idea of the "sowing logos" is found in the works of the Stoics, Middle Platonists, Numenius and Philo. Barnard, *St. Justin Martyr: The First and Second Apologies*, p. 15, states, "Philo's Logos is ultimately Stoicism or Middle Platonism blended with the Old Testament Word of God."

125 This is why Justin sees no inconsistency in quoting Scripture and Plato alike. All that is true in Plato is due to the Divine Logos: Osborn, "Justin's Response," p. 46.

(*1 Apol.* 44).

It followed that, far from being a novel upstart who appeared only recently on the historical stage, Jesus Christ was the pre-existent and eternal source of all truth (*2 Apol.* 10) working throughout all ages among all peoples and philosophies. Therefore, what appeared most recent was in fact most ancient, deserving of toleration and respect. Those ancients who acknowledged the *Logos* were, therefore, unwittingly participating in and acknowledging Jesus, the author of right reason, all along. Justin then made the audacious claim that all those in the past who lived by reason were Christians, including the Greek philosophers (*1 Apol.* 46), and that all truth, wherever it was, belonged to Christianity (*2 Apol.* 13).[126]

Finally, as distinct from paganism, which possessed only partial and contradictory truth because of a limited, indirect and impersonal participation in the *Logos*, Christianity was the full and definitive form of the truth because of its complete participation in the *Logos*. One could only possess more than a portion of the *Logos* by contemplating and receiving the whole *Logos* himself, who was Christ. "The Christian knows the sower, while the pagan knows the seed."[127] This Christ was sufficient, superseding the Stoics, Plato and even Socrates, all of whom contradicted each other (*2 Apol.* 10).

How did pagan dependence on the prophets practically differ from pagan dependence on the *Logos*? Firstly, Justin's argument of dependence on the prophets advocated an immediate, or

---

126 This is Justin's "imperialistic view of history" according to Droge, "Restoration of Philosophy," p. 315. In the opinion of Goodenough, *The Theology of Justin Martyr*, p. 108, the theory of the Christian character of all truth as presented by Justin was quite new to Christianity.

127 Osborn, "Justin Martyr and the Logos Spermatikos," p. 158. Chadwick, "Justin Martyr's Defence," p. 295, states, "Justin ingeniously insinuates that even the correct insights that the Greek philosophers possessed remained in the realm of potentiality and therefore need the gospel of Christ to elevate their aspiration to concrete reality."

proximate, influence of the writings of the prophets through borrowing upon pagan thought. On the other hand, Justin's *Logos*-Christ caused pagan dependence in two separate ways: first, as an immediate, or proximate, influence planting and inspiring seeds of truth in the reason of all men and women; second, as the primary and remote cause of truth mediated to paganism via the writings of the prophets. Justin credits the *Logos*-Christ with appearing to the patriarchs, inspiring Moses (*1 Apol.* 63) and the prophets (*1 Apol.* 36), who, in turn, inspired the Greek writers. (It followed that if Jesus Christ was the *Logos* who inspired Moses, then the Old Testament could be appropriated as a Christian library. This is one example of the way by which Justin's *Logos* speaks to more than one opponent). The second difference between the two lay in the fact that pagans dependent upon the prophets would have had at least some conscious and accurate knowledge of the identity of the writers they were borrowing from, while those ancients influenced by the spermatic *Logos* were totally oblivious to his real identity, that is, that he was Christ.

Appropriateness of the argument

Some ancients might have entertained Justin's theory that pagan philosophy borrowed from the prophets, in particular from Moses, as a number of them—including Hecataeus of Abdera, Cicero, Plutarch, Apuleius and Philostratus—were aware that Plato had visited Egypt[128]; also, Numenius of Apamea once asked, "What is Plato but Moses in Attic Greek?"[129] They may also

---

128 *Die Fragmente der griechischen Historiker* 264 F 25; *De Finibus Bonorum et Malorum.* 5.87; *De Iside et Osiride.* 354e; *De Dogmate Platonis* 1.3; *Vita Apollonii* 1.2. In addition to Plato, Orpheus, Homer, Pythagoras and Solon also visited Egypt to derive wisdom and learning: Droge, "Restoration of Philosophy," p. 311.
129 Numenius, F 8, *Numenius*, E. des Places (ed.), Paris: Les Belles Lettres, 1973, pp. 50-51. Justin may well have known of Numenius' reference: Droge, "Restoration of Philosophy," p. 312.

have encountered this form of argument from other writers, for example, the Jewish Peripatetic Aristobulus of Alexandria who during the second century BC proposed that Greek philosophers learned from Moses,[130] while Norris states that dependence "had been used already by Philo of Alexandria, from whom, directly or indirectly, Justin may well have derived it."[131] Similarly, Josephus in his work *Against Apion* (early second century AD) included lengthy calculations to establish the antiquity of the Jews and the dependence of the Greeks upon them.[132]

Nevertheless, it is highly doubtful that Justin's dependence argument would have been given serious consideration by anyone except his Christian readers, who would have valued it as supporting their claims of antiquity and originality. It was an assertion that rested on too many assumptions that needed to be proved by demonstrable evidence if ever it was to be received. First, concerning the doctrines he specified, Justin assumed that the teaching of the philosophers and the prophets were identical when in actual fact they were not. Second, Justin presupposed that where two individuals taught the same ideas the latter must have been dependent upon the earlier. Yet, nowhere did Justin offer any specific evidence to show how Plato, for example, came to know of and depend on Moses. Third, Justin took for granted that simply because Moses pre-dated Plato his was the more pure and authentic form of the teaching they shared, again without providing supporting evidence. What sounded like a convenient answer to explain dependence did not necessarily equate to a demonstrable and verifiable proof.

---

130 A. Dulles, *A History of Apologetics*, Ignatius Press, San Francisco, 2005, p. 29; Rhee, *Early Christian Literature*, p. 26.

131 R. A. Norris, *A Study in Justin Martyr, Irenaeus, Tertullian and Origen*, Adam & Charles Black, London, 1966, p. 40. Cf. L. G. Patterson, *God and History in Early Christian Thought: A Study of the Themes from Justin Martyr to Gregory the Great*, Adam & Charles Black, London, 1967, p. 34.

132 Chadwick, *Early Christian Thought*, p. 13. Justin's own calculations were somewhat inaccurate, placing the date of Moses as five thousand years before Christ (*1 Apol.* 31).

Justin's *Logos*-Christ was a Christian concept that had various counter-parts in the pagan philosophical world.[133] It therefore possessed greater potential to explain the origin of truth within paganism and make Christianity philosophically respectable than any simple appeal to purely Christian teachers and writings. Through the *Logos*-Christ Justin could address multiple objectives in his apologetical struggle. First, he highlighted the similarity of truths held by Christianity and paganism (while at the same time recognising that paganism had attained a significant degree of truth, even metaphysical truth). Second, he laid the same foundation for the source of these truths, thus bridging

---

133 L. W. Barnard, "The Logos Theology of St. Justin Martyr," *The Downside Review* 89 (1971), pp. 132-141 at p. 132. Osborn, "Justin Martyr and the Logos Spermatikos," p. 148, is convinced that Justin's idea of the *Logos Spermatikos* is chiefly derived from Stoicism. Barnard, *St. Justin Martyr*, p. 33, discounts Stoic influence on Justin's *Logos*, citing Justin's strong objection to Stoic teaching on materialism and fate, and arguing instead that Justin "was dependent on the earlier Christian use of the term and assumes that his readers will understand his ideas" (p. 99). Goodenough, *The Theology of Justin Martyr*, pp. 39-175, asserts that Justin was entirely dependent on Philo, "though popularized, diluted, intensely personalised... ." Andresen, "Justin und der mittlere Platonismus," *Zeitschrift für die neutestamentliche Wissenschaft* 44 (1952), pp.157-195 at pp. 170-177, points out the similarities between Justin's *Logos* and the concept of "implanted natural ideas" in Middle Platonism and admits the possibility of the latter's influence. R. M. Price, "'Hellenization' and Logos Doctrine in Justin Martyr," *Vigiliae Christianae* 42 (1988), pp. 18-23, regards such influence as "intrinsically plausible, in view of the Apologist's concern to make Christianity philosophically respectable." R. Holte, "Logos Spermatikos – Christianity and Ancient Philosophy according to St. Justin's Apologies," *Studia Theologica* 12 (1958), pp. 109-168 at p. 128, sees as probable the influence of Christ's parable of the Sower "to express conceptions that have really existed in the earlier Christian tradition." J. W. Pryor, "Justin Martyr and the Fourth Gospel," *The Second Century* 9 (1992), pp. 153-169 at pp. 160-163, reviews the possible sources and concludes that Justin was aware of John's *Logos* doctrine and that "the Johannine Logos is the starting point for his developed Christology." Finally, M. J. Edwards, "Justin's Logos and the Word of God," *Journal of Early Christian Studies* 3 (1995), pp. 261-280 at pp. 261-262, argues that his *Logos*-doctrine has roots "in the Biblical tradition." In summary, no one single influence can claim to be the sole source of Justin's *Logos*. Rather, he came to be familiar with *Logos*-doctrine in all its forms—first Stoic, then Middle-Platonic, then Philonic, finally Johannine—and combined them into the one *Logos*-Christ for his particular apologetical purposes.

the dividing line between the efforts of pagan and Christian philosophers to know truth. Third, he argued Christianity's possession of the fullness of truth, as against paganism's partial and imperfect possession. Fourth, he undermined the attack on Christianity's alleged novelty and obscure origins by identifying the ancient *Logos* with Christ. Based on this identification, Justin laid claim to all persons and truths held venerable from antiquity by paganism and Judaism. This last point was Justin's theology of history, which Chadwick[134] describes as his "distinctive and personal achievement … [Justin] sees the annals of humanity as a twofold story, sacred and profane, Jewish and Gentile, both being converging streams having their providential confluence in Christ and his universal gospel." However, for Justin there remained the difficulty of adducing the necessary evidence to prove his assertion that the *Logos* of paganism was actually the *Logos*-Christ of Christianity. In the end, it was a matter more of faith than demonstrable evidence and therefore an argument more appealing to Christians than anyone else.

Justin's employment of the *Logos* was also an appeal to paganism to enable his readers to understand the twofold and contradictory notion of God as both transcendent and yet immanent at the same time. Without such an understanding it would have been difficult for many pagans to accept philosophically the most central event for Christians, the incarnation of the Son of God. Justin's *Logos* made the unknowable God of the philosophers known to the world. Furthermore, Justin's *Logos* was not merely a mathematical or creative reason but love and reason coming together to sympathise, suffer with and redeem the creature. The *Logos* also served a similar purpose towards the Jews to whom it was blasphemy to assert that there was more than one God or that Jesus was a "second God." Therefore, the *Logos* safeguarded Christian monotheism while preserving a balance

---

134 Chadwick, "Justin Martyr's Defence," p. 297.

with both philosophical and Judaic monotheism.

Justin's explicit claims that the Greek philosophers who lived by reason were Christians, especially Socrates, and that all truth wherever existing belonged to Christianity would have been entertained by his internal audience but strongly resisted by outsiders. Undoubtedly, both claims would have appeared to educated pagans as preposterous, smacking especially of arrogance coming from a people who were so evidently low-class and uneducated. Concerning the former claim, it was one thing to say that Socrates and Christians both lived according to reason; it was certainly another to extend the argument to equate reason expressly and exclusively with Christianity. Socrates lived more than three centuries before Christ and left no extant writings that could assist in reconstructing his philosophy, his historical personality or whether he was remotely aware of the Jews let alone their supposed spiritual forerunners.[135] It was a claim chronologically akin to twentieth-century Marxists claiming Martin Luther as one of their own. Prudentially, Justin's purposes would have been better served by reversing his claims, arguing that as Christians lived according to reason through the aid of the *Logos* they were akin to the much-revered Socrates who was the ancient exemplar of right living and thought, and by that fact deserved acknowledgement, respect and tolerance as philosophers.

Osborn[136] suggests that by simultaneously arguing pagan dependence on the prophets and dependence on the *Logos* Justin introduced an obvious contradiction that seriously undermined his entire theory of dependence: "The Greek challenge to Christian maturity cannot be answered by both the spermatic

---

135 H. Hommel, "Sebasmata: Studien zur antiken Religionsgeschichte und zum frühen Christentum," vol. 2, WUNT 32, Tübingen, 1984, however, claims that there are surprising parallels between some sayings of Jesus and those of Socrates found in the works of later Greek writers.
136 Osborn, *Justin Martyr*, p. 313.

logos and the charge of Greek plagiarism. Either God has given seeds of truth or the Greeks have stolen them. Both accounts cannot be true." If Justin's "real opinion" was expressed in the *Logos* theory, as Harnack[137] suggests, then it would have been more advantageous if Justin had not raised the additional theory of plagiarism that was at best dubious and nigh impossible to prove.

However, a closer look at *1 Apol.* 44 reveals that Justin had no intention of referring all truths found in pagan philosophy to the prophets. He listed only "the immortality of the soul," "punishments after death" and the "contemplation of heavenly things" as being derived from them. Justin attributed other teachings about God himself, the falsity of idolatry and basic moral conceptions to the *Logos*. Consequently, the truth possessed by the pagan philosopher was derived partly from the Old Testament, partly from the *Logos* planting seeds of truth in all people. The two theories, therefore, did not contradict but complemented each other to present Christianity as the source and bearer of complete truth.

The Argument from Antiquity/Fulfilled Prophecy

Purpose: To recommend Christianity as the only safe and useful philosophy

Even if paganism had not borrowed from the prophets or had not been influenced by the Christ-*Logos*, Justin asserted that Judaeo-Christianity historically preceded the wisdom of the Graeco-Romans and by that fact could claim superiority according to the established principle that the older wisdom

---

137 Harnack, *Lehrbuch der Dogmengeschichte*, 1; 511, n. 1, taken from Osborn, *Justin Martyr*, p. 313, n. 7.

is the more authentic and trustworthy. Formally known as the argument of antiquity, Justin employed it to establish Christianity's rhetorical *ethos* and to counter the accusation that it was a newly-founded and dangerous novelty worthy only of the ignorant. As Young[138] observes, "Novelty was not prized in the Graeco-Roman society; for something to be true, it had to be ancient." Antiquity was therefore a vital part of the literary tradition of the day.

The argument from antiquity involved, *inter alia*, the inter-connected themes of the chronological age of Moses, the age of the Old Testament Scriptures, and argument from prophecy. The antiquity of Moses was already a well-accepted fact within Graeco-Roman traditions; nevertheless, Justin and Christian apologists after him were at pains to establish his priority with chronological research. If Moses was before Troy, Homer and Plato then it was Greek and Roman civilisation that was novel in comparison to the biblical culture. By establishing Christianity's antiquity, it could not be charged that anyone converting to it was offending the *mos maiorum*, or common fund of wisdom accumulated over the centuries that formed the foundation of society, and therefore Christianity on such a basis should be afforded respect, liberty and even consideration.[139]

The claim of Moses' antiquity naturally extends to his prophetic writings and those of the other prophets who lived before the advent of Graeco-Roman civilisation. Prophecy as a sub-section of antiquity so influenced Justin that he made it one of his cornerstone arguments. He considered fulfilled prophecy more convincing than any miracle (*1 Apol.* 30) and almost one-third of *1 Apology* is an *apodeixis* devoted to establishing

---

138 Young, "Greek Apologists of the Second Century," pp. 92-93.
139 It was considered the height of foolishness to substitute the classics of native tradition for an alien set of barbaric writings, and such foolishness became a key criticism of converts to Christianity, as evidenced in the later writings of Celsus: Young, "Greek Apologists of the Second Century," p. 93.

it (*1 Apol.* 31-53).[140] Proving the antiquity of Old Testament prophecies would give them added credibility; proving their fulfilment would compel assent to the divine nature of the Christian message.

Before his addressees, Justin appealed to "predictive prophecy," aware that such an argument would possess a certain force even for a pagan. However, he resorted little to allegorising, conscious that alleged hidden meanings would not be so persuasive to people yet to accept the Old Testament's status as the word of God.

Justin's hermeneutical excursus sought to establish Jesus' complete fulfilment of Old Testament expectations, that he is both the author and the latent sense of what is written. In the process Justin highlighted the following as prophecies fulfilled by Christ: his first coming in humility (*1 Apol.* 34), the virgin birth (*1 Apol.* 33), his healing of every sickness and disease (*1 Apol.* 31, 48), his raising of the dead (*1 Apol.* 48), his passion as the Just One (*1 Apol.* 50), his sacrifice as God's perfect paschal lamb (*1 Apol.* 31, 48), his resurrection and ascension (*1 Apol.* 42), his enthronement at God's right hand (*1 Apol.* 31), the disbelief of the Jews and the consequent destruction of Judea (*1 Apol.* 47-49), his current reign spreading out from Jerusalem through the apostles and the conversion of the nations (*1 Apol.* 31, 39, 42, 45, 53). Meanwhile, pagan fables were not supported by any prophecy (*1 Apol.* 54).

Furthermore, Justin argued that Christ himself foretold future things and his predictions had come to pass. These included the persecution of his followers (*1 Apol.* 12, 30, 31), the destruction of Jerusalem (*1 Apol.* 47), and the conversion

---

140 According to von Campenhausen, *The Fathers of the Greek Church*, p. 11, Justin's comprehensive compendium of Old Testament proof-texts confirming faith in Christ "has rarely been surpassed." Barnard, *St. Justin Martyr the First and Second Apologies*, p. 7, calls *1 Apol.* 23-53 "the more theological part of his work."

of the Gentiles (*1 Apol.* 49). Hence, Justin could boast, "We are more assured that all the things taught by Him are so, since whatever He predicted before is seen in fact coming to pass; and this is the work of God" (*1 Apol.* 12). The Jews, on the other hand, still failed to recognise the prophecies concerning Jesus or those made by him, bringing down God's punishment and the desolation of their nation (*1 Apol.* 47-49).

Taken together, evidence of antiquity and fulfilled prophecy constituted for Justin irresistible arguments in support of his protreptic and didactic objectives: judicial justice for the Christians; the abandonment of paganism for worship of the true God; and the reinforcement of Jesus' messianic credentials in the minds of Christians.

Appropriateness of the argument

As the truth of religion in Graeco-Roman society (in fact, in any ancient society) was substantially measured by its antiquity it was absolutely necessary that Justin present the credentials of Judaeo-Christianity in this regard. Without any presentation of evidence of ancestral heritage Christianity stood to retain its pariah status and condemnation as an affront to the *mos maiorum*.

Justin had the advantage of presenting an ancient starting point that was known and recognised by the pagans, namely Moses. Solomon was also widely recognised as a sage. The challenge that remained for Justin was to establish the historical link between these men and Jesus of Nazareth. While Christians frequented synagogues the pagans might have been willing to entertain Justin's arguments. However, it was a task complicated by the Jewish rejection of Jesus—a fact that certainly did not escape the notice of the Romans—and perhaps severely wounded by the eventual 'parting of the ways' between

Christians and Jews. Furthermore, some Romans were aware that the teachings of Moses and Jesus differed in significant areas (for example, revenge, divorce) and that Moses did not expect the messiah to be an incarnation of God. To dissociate Jesus entirely from Moses would have left him and his followers wallowing as nothing more than the newest of all movements and hence the furthest away from the truth disclosed by the divine powers at the beginning of human civilisation.

Another problem lay in the Graeco-Roman conception of culture. Those who did not possess the requisite language, ideals and values were considered barbarians. Many Romans considered the Jewish culture as perverse and disgusting, the Jewish religion tasteless and mean. By laying claim to antiquity through Judaism, Justin ran the risk of associating Christians with Jews as cultural barbarians. Unfortunately, Christians who rejected outright Graeco-Roman *paideia*, philosophy, customs, etc., only gave weight to this charge, hampering the efforts of those who sought for Christianity a respectful hearing and the protection of the empire's laws.

Justin's appeal to Old Testament prophecy was in line with the recognition of oracle by pagan rhetoricians. Aristotle included interpreters of oracles as valuable sources of evidence about the future while Quintilian called this type of evidence *"divina,"* that is, "divine." The argument from prophecy was afforded the status of "supernatural witness" and was used especially in pagan conversion narratives. Philosophers themselves were known to serve as prophets in important places of oracles. Tertullian refers to the widespread influence of pagan oracles during the second and early third centuries.[141] Even Marcus Aurelius in his *Meditations* (1.17) confessed to "receiving help" through dreams and from the oracle of Caieta. As a youth

---

141 Tertullian, *Treatise on the Soul*, 46 (c. AD 206-207).

he had also been a student in the priestly college of Salii and was given the status of *vates* (prophet).[142] On the basis of such evidence it is reasonable to assume that Marcus would not have simply dismissed prophecy *per se* as contrary to intelligence or philosophy but would have valued its private and political importance, at least when prophecy was based on traditional Graeco-Roman religion. (There is also evidence from the third century suggesting the approved status of eastern oracles[143]). Justin would have been aware of the extent to which prophecy was valued in popular, philosophical and political circles and accordingly calculated that his pagan readers would be impressed by an extensive argument based on 'fulfilled' ancient eastern prophecy.

Justin relied heavily on Old Testament prophecies, in part, because they were readily accessible. Jesus himself was not. Arguing from fulfilled prophecy enabled Justin to link the foundational and climactic events of Christianity with books of undoubted age and venerability, thereby satisfying the rigorous demands of antiquity and truth. Justin's tactic also enabled him to counter the charges that the Christians believed simply out of blind faith and betrayed their ancestral roots, namely, Judaism.

Nonetheless, in the debate with paganism any argument that Jesus fulfilled Old Testament prophecy would have been meaningless, rendering Justin's whole presentation flawed, if the addressees did not regard the prophecies as valuable oracles worth fulfilling in the first place. For Justin's proof-from-prophecy argument to succeed he needed to establish the credibility of the Hebrew prophets in the minds of pagans who did not accept the Old Testament's inspiration by the *Logos*. To this end, Justin associated the martyred prophets of the Old Testament with the pagan oracles who were popular and

---

142 Birley, *Marcus Aurelius*, pp. 103-104.
143 Guerra, "The Conversion of Marcus Aurelius," p. 185.

respected among the Romans. Those who sought knowledge of good things in the books of Hystaspes, the Sybil or the prophets were all sentenced to death (*1 Apol.* 44). In this way Justin hoped to extend to the prophets Roman deference to traditional pagan oracle. As to why the prophets should be believed over pagan oracles, Justin did not adduce any specific arguments to prove that the prophets were divinely inspired, choosing instead to engage in one-upmanship, declaring that Moses and the prophets were "older than all writers" (*1 Apol.* 54), a fact of antiquity that entitled him to precedence over all others. Ultimately, Justin's reason for believing the prophets was beyond reason, beyond proof. One believed on faith that the prophets were witnesses to the truth and spoke only on matters they had seen and heard. If prophecy was fulfilled it was self-evidently true—and the prophecies concerning the messiah had been fulfilled in Christ.

However, Justin's appeal to the venerable age and eastern origin of the prophets alone could not fully satisfy the ancient canons of logic, which demanded demonstration before consent, rather than simple axiomatic acceptance. As evidenced by Celsus (who charged that thousands of others could have fulfilled the same prophecies more thoroughly than Jesus of Nazareth[144]) the Romans were not going to accept argument from prophecy simply by faith; it was necessary to persuade them by evidence. As the mystery religions could point to their own oracular utterances and supporting proofs Justin needed to adduce historical evidence that the prophets did actually utter ancient prophecy and that Jesus of Nazareth in fact fulfilled such prophecy. Justin adduced that the prophecies in question were enshrined in ancient books written initially in Hebrew and later translated into Greek under the orders of Ptolemy of Egypt

---

144 Origen, *Against Celsus*, 7.18.

when he endeavoured to assemble his universal library.[145] The antiquity of these prophecies, declared Justin, could therefore be easily verified and their knowledge beyond the confines of Judea established. Justin was on safe ground relying on age-old foresight, as it was the generally accepted pagan criteria for determining the correctness of prophetic writings. As to whether these same utterances were fulfilled, the Gospels—particularly Matthew and Luke, or "Memoirs" (ἀπομνημονεύματα) as Justin called them—were reliable records of their complete and exact historical fulfilment in the life of Jesus Christ.[146] However, as Chadwick[147] notes, Justin was inhibited in his ability to produce the necessary evidence of fulfilment as he had "not yet got a book called the New Testament which he [could] thrust into the hands of benevolent inquirers." This is perhaps why Justin felt obliged at times (*1 Apol.* 34, 35, 68) to appeal to external evidence held in the Roman's own records (such as the records of Cyrenius' census and reports sent by Pontius Pilate to Rome) of Christ's birth in Bethlehem and later crucifixion in Jerusalem and to the contemporary devastation and loss of Judea as a living testimony (*1 Apol.* 47, 53).

Ultimately, Justin's proof-from-prophecy argument towards pagans was a sword that could cut both ways and was vulnerable to yielding only ambiguous results.

---

145 Justin repeats the *Letter of Aristeas* (late 3rd century BC), which describes how the Septuagint was carefully preserved and later ordered translated into Greek by Ptolemy for the use and guidance of all. Many of the Septuagint prophecies and their 'proofs' used by Justin were probably committed to separate writings/anthologies before his time. Justin's use of these anthologies, or 'testimonies,' may account for his attribution of texts to the wrong authors in *1 Apol.* 35, 51, 53, *Dial.* 12, 14 and 49: Osborn, *Justin Martyr*, pp. 114-115. The production of testimonies steadily grew in number after the end of the Apostolic age: Barnard, *St. Justin Martyr the First and Second Apologies*, p. 9; Chadwick, "Justin Martyr's Defence," pp. 281-282.
146 Justin was certainly aware of these two Gospels, as evidenced elsewhere in *Dial.* 99, 100, 101, 103, 104, 105, 106, 107.
147 Chadwick, "Justin Martyr's Defence," p. 283.

The Argument from Miracles

Purpose: To recommend Christianity as the only safe and useful philosophy

Crucial to Justin's protreptic/evangelistic endeavours towards his pagan audience was the provision of some form of "ocular manifestation" to demonstrate that a crucified Jewish felon was in reality the Son of God and the king and judge of all humanity. The realm of miracle could supply the demonstrable evidence and was a domain recognised by all forms of pagan piety.

Justin viewed miracles in terms of power validating the claims of exclusive monotheism over the polytheism of the pagan world. More to the point, the miracles wrought by Jesus of Nazareth during his lifetime, and those still worked in his name by his contemporary followers, supported Jesus' rhetorical *ethos* and validated the thesis of his superiority and that of the religion which he established (*1 Apol.* 22).

In his efforts to persuade the emperors of such Justin mentioned a number of the past miracles of Christ, including the curing of the blind, lame and paralysed (*1 Apol.* 22), the raising of the dead (*1 Apol.* 31), the opening of the tongues of the mute, and the cleansing of lepers (*1 Apol.* 48). These miracle accounts, especially those of resurrection, were sufficient in Justin's view to convince any listener of the authentic and superior power of the Christian God and to abandon paganism.

Not only did Jesus perform such works; according to Justin he did so in fulfilment of ancient prophecy (*1 Apol.* 31, 48). The prophecies predicting Christ's miracles were "older than all the writers who have lived" (*1 Apol.* 23), and therefore deserving of respect and belief, while alleged pagan miracles (particularly those associated with the Asclepius cult)[148] were either without evidence (*1 Apol.* 54), simple fabrications (*1 Apol.* 23) or associated with shameful deeds such as parricide, sodomy, adultery (*1 Apol.* 21; *2 Apol.* 12). For believers such as Justin, the Christian miracle itself was the revelation, the unqualified manifestation establishing the absolute uniqueness and truth of Christ and Christianity, placing the onus on the authorities and the general public to heed the demand for judicial justice and even reconsider their allegiance to paganism.

Appropriateness of the argument

Prima facie, Justin's appeal to Jesus' miracles as evidence of Christianity's exclusive truth and superiority had significant potential for success as miracle stories and healing cults were thoroughly familiar to the ancient world in general and, similarly to Justin, the popular Graeco-Roman mind conceived miracles in terms of the manifestation of a divine power greater than others. Even though the intensity of belief in miracles rose and fell from age to age, demonstrating the extraordinary always remained the most common and persuasive means of eliciting the conversion of individuals, households and crowds in the ancient world and belief in 'divine-men' (θεῖοι ανδρες) who worked miracles was a persistent phenomenon among pagans: Melampas and Abaris (seventh century BC); Aristeas and Pythagoras (sixth century BC); and Empedocles (fifth century BC). In Justin's time, even the emperor Marcus Aurelius, despite writing that he generally distrusted reports of miracle workers, incantations and exorcisms (*Med.* 1.6), was willing to

---

148 From the first century AD onwards some of the most significant intellectuals of paganism became ardent devotees of Asclepius, including the orators Aelius Aristides and Libanius. G. Theissen, *The Miracle Stories of the Early Christian Tradition*, Fortress Press, Philadelphia, 1983, p. 270, observes that the level of pietistic worship given to Asclepius made him a serious "rival of Christ."

acknowledge certain reports of miracles as credible, given his permission for the issuance of a coin in AD 173 commemorating the "Rain Miracle" that delivered the Roman soldiers fighting the Sarmatians in Germany.

Nevertheless, there was still risk in Justin's appeal to miracles as proof of the truth of Christ's claims. The contemporary Graeco-Roman market-place was already saturated with claims of miracles allegedly performed by members of any and all religions, social groups and philosophies. Claims of another wonder-worker performing purported prodigies would have excited some among the common masses but would have been received with scepticism by the educated and philosophical elite. There was also the real risk of being associated with magic, a charge seriously scandalous enough to risk a charge of sedition, a capital offence.[149] Christ had long since been variously labelled by Jews and pagans as a magician (μάγος) and deceiver (λαοπλάνος) who performed his work by magical art (μαγικὴ τέχνη) or recipes (μαθήματα), and whose healings and resurrections were magical illusions (φαντασία μαγική). The source of Jesus' magical powers, or γοητεία, was said to be Egypt. Later Jewish writings gave this as the rationale for his execution.[150] Furthermore, Justin's contemporaries did not themselves witness any of the claimed signs of Christ; rather, they were confronted with only reports of those signs, which did not amount to irrefutable, objective demonstration. If Justin was to make an impression on any strata of Graeco-Roman society it was incumbent upon him to supply hard empirical evidence substantiating Christ's miraculous powers while simultaneously distinguishing such from the black arts.

---

149 According to Dulles, *A History of Apologetics*, p. 30, "generally speaking, the miracles of Jesus occupy a very subordinate place in the apologetics of the first three centuries. The Christians did not want their faith confused with pagan thaumaturgy."
150 Babylonian Talmud tractate, Sanhedrin 43a.

Aware of these obstacles, Justin adduced two examples of contemporary miracles evident before the eyes of the pagan world: firstly, the progressive conversion of the world (again in fulfilment of prophecy: *1 Apol.* 41, 42); secondly, Christian exorcists who cast out evil spirits (*2 Apol.* 3) otherwise impervious to the efforts of exorcists employing incantations and drugs (*2 Apol.* 6). There were benefits in mentioning such, for as Remus[151] comments, "[t]he relation between then and now was reciprocal and mutually reinforcing: the extraordinary happenings in the Jesus story made extraordinary happenings in the present seem plausible, and vice versa."

The Graeco-Roman period was one in which interest in magic flourished. Pliny[152] wrote, "There is indeed nobody who does not fear to be spell-bound by imprecations." Magic was opposed not because of the risk of fraud, but because it was believed to obtain results through the agency of evil powers.[153] Remus[154] outlines the difficulty in determining what, if any, were the objective criteria employed by second-century polemicists on both sides of the divide to distinguish between 'magic' and 'miracle.' The demarcation often simply involved social and cultural judgements, upon which each side accused the other that "your magic is my miracle, and vice versa." Aune[155] gives his criteria for demarcation as follows: (i) magic is manipulative, religion is supplicative; (ii) magic seeks specific goals, religion is an end in itself; (iii) magic seeks to benefit the individual, religion the group; (iv) magic adopts a professional-client relationship,

---

151 H. Remus, *Pagan-Christian Conflict over Miracle in the Second Century*, The Philadelphia Patristic Foundation, Philadelphia, 1983, ch. 9, p. 152.

152 Pliny, *Natural History*, 28.4. Translated by W. H. S. Jones, vol. 8. The Loeb Classical Library, ed. G.P. Goold, Harvard University Press, Cambridge, Mass., 1963.

153 N. Janowitz, "Magic in the Roman Empire: Pagans, Jews, and Christians," in *Religion in the First Christian Centuries*, Routledge, New York, 2001, p. 3.

154 Harold Remus, "Magic or Miracle? Some Second-Century Instances," *The Second Century* 2 (1982), pp. 127-156.

155 D. E. Aune, "Magic in Early Christianity," *ANRW* II.23.2: pp. 1507-1557 at p. 1515.

religion a shepherd-flock relationship; and (v) magic tends to act impersonally without emotion, religion makes a greater use of emotion and evokes awe and worship directed towards a divine being.

The fact that Christians were counter-cultural and held a marginal place in society rendered them more susceptible to the accusation that their 'miracles' were but magic, since magic was clandestine by nature. Any charge that alleged miracles were rather works of magic were normally supported by evidence that the wonder-worker in question employed magical paraphernalia, spells or incantations of the type evidenced in the over one thousand 'magical papyri' discovered during the nineteenth century and used in Greek-speaking communities of pre-Christian Egypt.[156] It appears that Justin was conscious of this connection and therefore sought to distinguish Christian exorcism miracles from "those who used incantations and drugs" (*2 Apol.* 6). Rather, Christians used "the name of Jesus Christ," giving weight to the alternative that only divine power was the principle cause of his phenomena. However, such evidence could easily have been contested by any pagan aware of the story of Jesus' healing of the blind man in John 9, which occurred only after Jesus repeatedly applied mud mixed with his own spit to his eyes. Furthermore, the very objects and practices used in Christian liturgical and sacramental worship—such as the cross, water, oil, bread, wine, laying of hands—could without difficulty have been regarded by pagans as similar to substances commonly employed elsewhere by magicians. Justin did not produce all the available evidence to distinguish Jesus' miracles from the magical for his imperial audience. Nowhere, for example, does he outline any of the occasions when Jesus performed prodigies in his own name (indicating thereby his

---

156 See C. L. Blomberg, *The Historical Reliability of the Gospels*, Inter-Varsity Press, Leicester, 1987, p. 86.

divine authority) and only by his word (for example, Mark 5:41; Luke 7:14; John 11:43).

Whether or not Jesus acted only through word, object or both, it remained for Justin to prove that he was not just another fraudulent 'holy-man' (γόης) successfully deceiving the credulous through illusion. In most cases, it was sufficient for the wonder-worker merely to work his wonders to gain credit among the common people. They were not always equipped to distinguish between the authentic and the charlatan. For Justin, it was axiomatic that claims of extraordinary phenomena, whether performed by Christ or by others in his name, were authentic miracles (*1 Apol.* 23). However, what was axiomatic for Justin was not so for the intellectual Graeco-Roman religious mind that sought to discern the frauds from the genuine, as evidenced in the works of such writers as Lucian, Celsus, Oenomaus of Gadara and Sextus Empiricus. Justin should have specifically held up Christ's virtuous life and those of his followers as remote proof dispelling the possibility of fraud. He also could have made more of the fact that Jesus' miracles were usually for the poor and afflicted and that he never sought to obtain any material or worldly benefit for such. Finally, precise facts could have been provided of particular miracles to show how they were devoid of the immorality and sordid details Justin highlighted in pagan wonders (*1 Apol.* 21; *2 Apol.* 12).

Furthermore, even if Jesus was a genuine miracle-worker, why should he be regarded as the unique Son of God when pagans believed there were other 'divine-men,' some even contemporary with him, who allegedly performed similar wonders?[157] The linking by Justin of Christ's miracles with

---

157 Such as Apollonius of Tyana, who, according to his biographer Philostratus (*The Life of Apollonius of Tyana* 4.45), showed great wisdom as a child, performed notable healings as an adult, predicted the future, performed exorcisms, appeared to his followers after his death, and later ascended into heaven.

the fulfilment of prophecy was his "strongest and surest" (*1 Apol.* 30) means of reinforcing their divine origin and Christ's claim to divine Sonship. Of course, Justin had to first establish through objective proofs the credibility of the prophets to pagan outsiders before proceeding any further. This he attempted to do extensively in *1 Apol.* 31-53. The prophets would not be received as oracles by the pagans simply because they were commonly accepted as such by Christians or even Jews.

To establish monotheism in the minds of his audience, it was both inevitable and crucial that Justin contest the claims of alleged pagan miracles. The pagan gods had to be shown up as impotent, non-existent, or at least that the claimed miracles were the work of demons seeking either to maintain their general hold over humanity (*1 Apol.* 69) or to deter anyone from converting to Christianity (*1 Apol.* 54). Justin's corpus of criticisms of pagan miracles is noteworthy in the way it echoed the traditional pagan critique of them. In so framing his arguments, Justin minimised the risk of being regarded as an alien and dangerous voice against the popular and accepted piety. Rather, he could show that he was not too dissimilar from the respected intellectual-philosophical-rational elite who preferred to believe in alternative (albeit scientific or natural) causes for pagan miracle claims. Furthermore, in reciting the shameful actions of the pagan deities that were said to be the power behind miracles, Justin would have struck a sympathetic chord with those Stoics and other philosophers who shared a similar revulsion at such behaviour.

Finally, Justin's argument that paganism could adduce no demonstrable evidence to confirm their miracle claims was simply a turning-of-the-tables on those who insisted that Christ's miracles could carry weight only with those who actually witnessed them. In the most basic terms, Justin was only insisting on the same standard of proof pagan critics required of Christian miracles.

Chapter 6

Justin's Apologetical Arguments in *Dialogue*

In Chapter Four, it was concluded that Justin wrote *Dialogue* to achieve the following purposes:

(i)   he wanted others to know of and follow him into the "only safe and useful philosophy," namely Christianity, that is, to convert unattached Gentiles who were broadly sympathetic to both Judaism and Christianity.

(ii) to provide a helpful internal sourcebook for study by Christians for apology to Jews.

(iii) to combat Judaising Christians who wished to foist law-keeping on Gentile Christians in Rome.

(iv) to counter Marcion and his rejection of the Torah and the God of the Old Testament.

The opposition of the Jews, Judaisers and Marcionites to the claims of mainstream Christianity necessitated the development of arguments by Justin exclusively in response to them. In *Dialogue*, Justin employed four major arguments, namely, Superiority, Fulfilled Prophecy, Miracles, and True Israel, the first three paralleling arguments in his *Apologies*. This latter point is understandable, considering the fact that Justin was competing for Gentile converts with Judaism, a religion whose adherents practised strict legal and moral observances and deeply believed in both prophecy and miracles.

The process of outline and analysis employed in Chapter Five to determine appropriateness will again be used to assess Justin's most outstanding arguments in *Dialogue*.

The Argument from Superiority

Purpose: To convert unattached Gentiles to the "only sure and useful philosophy"

In the opening chapters of *Dialogue* Justin described how prior to his conversion to Christianity he had moved among philosophers and journeyed through a range of philosophies— Stoic, Peripatetic, Pythagorean and Platonic—in his quest for truth (*Dial.* 2). In the course of his narration, however, Justin only scantily compared the distinct teachings of these various philosophies. Of these schools Justin gave greatest attention to Platonism, probably as he had spent considerable time with it, it was the most popular, and it was the closest of the Greek academies to Christianity. Nevertheless, Justin would engage in a forensic examination of competing ideas, as it was one of his primary objectives to establish the superiority of Christianity as a philosophy for the protreptic purpose of converting unattached Gentiles to the latter.

In outlining his 'journey through philosophy,' Justin began with a declaration that "philosophy is indeed one's greatest possession, and is most precious in the sight of God ... sent down to men," and stated that those who bestowed attention upon it "are holy men" (*Dial.* 2).[158] Chadwick[159] describes this attitude as Justin's "positive optimism towards classical philosophy," in contrast to his "radical rejection of the pagan religious tradition." Schönborn[160] comments:

> Behind this effort [of the early Apologists] at a positive evaluation of pre-Christian philosophies there does not lie a superficial apologetical interest, but the fundamental conviction that the truth is one and that at least traces of the truth are to be found everywhere.

At an earlier point Justin even boldly declared that the true duty of philosophy was to "inquire about the divine" *(Dial.* 1). In other words, philosophy and Christianity shared the same ultimate end—studying and understanding the highest truth, which is God. Christianity was for Justin the natural fulfilment of the best of Greek philosophy as well as the Old Law of the Jews. Patterson[161] sums it up in these terms: "Justin's view depends for its cogency on his assumption that God's action in the present course of events is at once the fulfilment of his promises to Israel and the goal of the Greek philosophical quest."

However, when speaking of his conversion to Christianity Justin stated that it was a conversion to the only philosophy that was "sure and useful" (*Dial.* 8). He regarded the other philosophies as unsatisfactory except for the seeds of truth that had fallen on them. Justin believed that the "primordial philosophy" was one and had been sent down by God. The very fact that there existed a plurality of contradictory philosophical schools under different names was evidence enough that

---

158 These words echo Plato, *Timaeus* 47 ab and Philo, *De Opificio Mundi* 54.
159 Chadwick, "Justin Martyr's Defence," p. 294.
160 C. Schönborn, "Does the Church Need Philosophy?," p. 343.
161 Patterson, *God and History in Early Christian Thought*, p. 36.

corruption had crept in. The errors and contradictions in pagan philosophy were not due to those who first received it but were produced by those coming afterwards who understood only a part of what the masters taught and then handed down their own limited and divergent interpretations (*Dial.* 1). These errors existed in all philosophies without exception. For example, while Plato and Christ agreed on many points, Plato believed in the pre-existence and transmigration of the soul (*Dial.* 4) and that the soul was naturally immortal instead of being dependent for existence on God's will (*Dial.* 5, 6). Justin considered the Stoics first-rate on ethics, but disastrously wrong in their materialism, pantheism, and fatalism.

Justin held that the "primordial philosophy" was now only to be found in the books of the Old Testament prophets with Scripture providing a coherent statement of doctrine answering the philosophical questions concerning the beginning and end of all things (*Dial.* 7). In fulfilment of the prophets, Christianity was the restoration of the primordial philosophy (being corrective and supplementary) and Christians were philosophers in the only "safe and useful" philosophy. All this Justin said with bluntness and decision.

For Justin, becoming a Christian therefore meant passing beyond the partial truth of Platonism to a superior and perfect truth. However, it did not involve making a clear break with Greek philosophy, the best elements of which prepared the way for the coming of the Gospel. As Denning-Bolle[162] states, "[hence], it was necessary to demonstrate this new philosophy's continuation with the revered philosophy of the Greeks." Therefore, Greek metaphysics proved to be both the common factor and the bridge that enabled Justin's smooth move from Platonism to Christianity.

---

162 Denning-Bolle, "Christian Dialogue as Apologetic," p. 505.

Christianity was the source of perfect truth for Justin because the prophets alone had seen and heard God (*Dial.* 7). Truth could only be known immediately. The philosophers could not speak truthfully of God as they had neither seen him nor encountered anyone who had seen him. This was the reason why philosophy had broken down and was now wrong with respect to both particular and ultimate things. As pagan philosophical subtlety could not give perfect knowledge of the truth the philosophers had to give way to the prophets. Justin advocated Christianity as the only safe and useful philosophy because through it he had received a direct and perfect knowledge of the truth.

Appropriateness of the argument

Justin addressed *Dialogue* specifically to one person, Marcus Pompeius *(Dial.* 142), presumably a Gentile considering the competing claims of Christianity and Judaism. In view of the length of *Dialogue* Pompeius must have been a man of some learning and may well have had a background similar to Justin's. That is, he may have been a pagan possessing a notable level of philosophical knowledge and adherence to metaphysical truth. That being the case, to secure his conversion Justin would have needed to pursue the following three ends: (i) illustrate that Christianity possessed wisdom of the kind to qualify it as a philosophy; (ii) counter the negative attitude that many Christians held and expressed towards philosophy; and (iii) assert that Christianity was superior to all other philosophies. It was possible for Justin to achieve all three objectives by a well-developed argument in favour of (iii).

By giving praise to philosophy and philosophers in *Dialogue* 1 and 2 Justin engaged in an appropriate starting measure to make Pompeius confident that Christianity did not totally disdain the natural wisdom of the ancients. The introduction of the further claim of Christianity's philosophical superiority, however, was one that needed to be simultaneously supported with substantive and demonstrable evidence. Justin could have sufficiently discharged this obligation by presenting evidence of the moral life of Christians. As Wilken[163] states, "[l]ong before the appearance of Christianity philosophy had become, not so much a way of thinking about the world, but a way of teaching men to live in the world." Hence, Justin declared, "we cultivate piety, justice, brotherly charity, faith, and hope" (*Dial.* 110). The first three of these terms parallel Seneca, who wrote that "religion, piety, justice never depart from the side of philosophy."[164] It is debatable, though, whether Justin produced sufficient evidence in *Dialogue* to buttress his claim of superiority. Unlike *1 Apology*, Justin did not systematically detail specific aspects of Christian life and worship, making only general claims about Christian righteousness through baptism (*Dial.* 16), how Christ obtained righteousness for Christians (*Dial.* 28) and how Christians were more faithful to God than the Jews (*Dial.* 131).

Arguing that Christianity was the only "sure and useful" philosophy would have appealed to sophisticated Christians engaging with pagans considering monotheism and debating Jews about Jesus. Not only did Justin not mention Judaism as one of the philosophies, he did not even present it as a remote option for consideration. Such would have contributed to the process of Christian self-definition by making sharper the contrast with Judaism. On the other hand, Justin would have faced opposition from 'traditional' Christians who had a positive distaste for philosophy as pagan belief. Their viewpoint was best summed up in the oft-quoted line from Tertullian, written a generation after Justin's death, "What has Athens to do with

---

163 Wilken, "Toward a Social Interpretation of Early Christian Apologetics," p. 443.
164 Wilken, "Toward a Social Interpretation of Early Christian Apologetics," p. 446.

Jerusalem?"[165] These Christians would have regarded Justin's idea as a dangerous innovation from one just lately familiar with the Christian faith. Nevertheless, 'suspicion at home' has no bearing on the appropriateness of an argument vis-à-vis the intended audience; and over time philosophical superiority was eventually recognised by the majority of Christians as a valuable argument for establishing the credentials of Christianity.

Justin's claim of Christian philosophical superiority was one that could have seriously appealed only to pagans already considering either Judaism or Christianity. Undoubtedly, most other pagans within the Graeco-Roman paideia would have been left aghast at such a claim. How could uneducated slaves and women demanding unquestioning and irrational faith claim knowledge of God, the origin of the world, and the supposed depravity of the gods of the pagans? Only one pagan philosopher during the first two centuries AD—namely Galen—was even remotely prepared to accord Christianity the status of a philosophy at all, let alone a superior philosophy.[166] Christianity did not yet have a pedigree of venerable teachers as lengthy as, for example, that of Stoicism, the most influential philosophy in Rome during the mid-second century. The Stoics in Justin's time could already point to a succession of teachers going back five centuries: Zeno, Cleanthes, Chryssipus,

---

165 Tertullian, *The Demurrer Against the Heretics* 7.9. Whatever Tertullian truly believed about the value of philosophy, it suited his rhetorical purpose in this treatise to express a negative opinion. See Dunn, *Tertullian*, pp. 31-34.

166 In his work, *On the Pulse* 2.4, Galen polemically complains of certain physicians and philosophers who have capitulated to blind faith "as if one had come into the school of Moses and Christ and heard talk of undemonstrated laws." Yet, elsewhere he says of the Christians, "For they include not only men and women who refrain from cohabiting all through their lives; and they also number individuals who, in self-discipline and self-control in matters of food and drink, have attained a pitch not inferior to that of genuine philosophers." Cited by S. Mason, "Philosophai: Graeco-Roman, Judean and Christian," in *Voluntary Associations in the Graeco-Roman World*, edd. J. S. Kloppenborg and S.G. Wilson, Routledge, London and New York, 1996, pp. 31-55 at p. 52.

Poseidonius, Musonius Rufus, Epictetus, and Seneca. Other philosophical schools could have produced a list of similar length. The Christians, on the other hand, could point to no pool of 'philosophers' of their own. The reactions of the 'astonished' among the pagan philosophical milieu would have ranged from disdainful dismissals to demands for a continuation of the violent repression of 'presumptuous upstarts' whose 'outrageous claims' threatened to supplant the long held traditional beliefs that gave the empire its strength.

Nevertheless, there was still value in Justin's superiority rhetoric. Graeco-Romans were never more conscious of their need for truth than in the second century. The empirical evidence of the failure of existing philosophies to provide a comprehensive answer to all life's questions justified the advent of another school of thought in the minds of some. The real difficulty lay not in the claim of superiority itself but the context in which it was made, that is, a Graeco-Roman society so prejudiced against the Christians that it was unwilling to accept even the possibility that they deserved intellectual recognition let alone grant them a respectful hearing. In any case, proving that Christianity was a philosophy was not a guarantee of acceptance as there were still enough philosophers, especially Stoics, who met with rebuke, censure or exile.

The Argument from Fulfilled Prophecy

Purpose: To convert unattached Gentiles, fortify Christians, combat Judaising Christians, counter Marcionism

The Jews, like the Gentiles who surrounded them, were a people who fervently believed in prophecy. For many, some of the most revered prophecies contained in the Old Testament Scriptures related to the coming of the Messiah.[167] Anyone claiming Messiah status needed to provide evidence of fulfilment of these prophecies to win acceptance. It was, therefore, an essential test Christians needed to satisfy with respect to Jesus.

Justin in the prologue to *Dialogue* indicated that he was converted to Christianity by arguments that included 'proof from prophecy'—that is, proofs that Jesus of Nazareth was the one who fulfilled the centuries-old prophecies of the Old Testament. The 'old man' in *Dial.* 7 presented the argument to him as follows:

> A long time ago, … long before the time of those so-called philosophers, there lived blessed men who were just and loved by God, men who spoke through the inspiration of the Holy Spirit and predicted events that would take place in the future, which events are now taking place. We call these men the prophets … Their writings are still extant, and whoever reads them with the proper faith will profit greatly in his knowledge of the origin and end of things, and of any other matter that a philosopher should know … the happenings that

---

167 Second-century Jews held diverse beliefs with respect to the Messiah. The Jewish daily prayer of the Eighteen Benedictions (both the Babylonian and Palestinian recensions) speaks explicitly of the throne of David. For example, the fifteenth benediction of the Babylonian recension states, "Make the Branch of David to sprout quickly, and let his horn be exalted by thy salvation." Rabbi Akiba hailed the leader of the second revolt in AD 132-135, Simon Bar-Cochba, as the Messiah. Various Targums (*Tg. Onq.*, *Tg. Ps-J.*, and *Tg. Neof.*, speak of "the king" and "the Messiah," "the Messiah and a sceptre," "a redeemer and a chief." However, some Jews believed that the expectations of a radical and definitive change brought about by God did not necessarily require human or angelic agents of deliverance. The Mishnah mentions the Messiah only in two places (*m. Ber.* 1:5 and *m. Sota* 9:15). Some Rabbis preferred to give an historical rather than messianic interpretation to Old Testament prophecies. To quote R. Hillel, "There shall be no Messiah for Israel, because they have already enjoyed him in the days of Hezekiah" (*Sanh.* 99a). Christian writings placing a strong emphasis on Jewish hope for the Messiah should be read against a background of debate between Jews and Christians about Jesus, whom Christians believed to be the Christ.

have taken place and are now taking place force you to believe their words.

Proof from prophecy so influenced Justin that 134 chapters of *Dialogue* are an *apodeixis* devoted to establishing this argument. Justin's principal idea was that the ancient prophets conveyed divine truths and that the Old Testament paved the way for the new Law, instituted by Christ. The Old Testament was Justin's 'sacred book,' more authoritative than any record, and the foundation for the authority of the life and sayings of Jesus Christ.

Justin asserted the Christian claim to the Old Testament via fulfilled prophecy in pursuit of the following respective protreptic, didactic and forensic aims: to upstage the Jews who regarded it as their own and so influence unattached Gentiles in the missionary competition for God-fearers; to assert against Judaising Christians that circumcision was merely a type foreshadowing baptism; to fortify Christians engaging Jews in debate about the authenticity of Jesus' mission; and to maintain the canonical status of the Old Testament against the Gnostics and Marcionites who rejected it as a work of the inferior God of the Jews. As when writing to the emperors, there was a need for Justin to establish an association between Jesus and Moses; however, there was no equivalent need to attack mythological fables, but rather contrary Jewish interpretations of prophecy.

According to Skarsaune[168], the prophecies concerning Christ and their fulfilment "are not, strictly speaking, part of the Christian message, but they authenticate the message. The prophecies are proved to be true by their fulfilment, and Christ is shown to come from God because of the prophecies. Christ and the prophets authenticate each other." In contrast with the Apologies, Justin assumes the right before his Gentile

---

168 Skarsaune, "The Conversion of Justin Martyr," p. 58.

and Christian readers of *Dialogue* to freely rely on "Rabbinic and Philonic allegorical and typological methods of scriptural interpretation accepted within Christianity, combined with a rabbinical thoroughness in assembling apparently rare clues and hidden affinities"[169], to give the argument its full and classic development.

In seeking to establish Jesus' messianic credentials Justin put forward the following as prophecies fulfilled by him: the coming of his precursor, Elijah (*Dial.* 51), his first coming in humility (*Dial.* 78), the virgin birth (*Dial.* 43, 84), the visit of the wise men (*Dial.* 77), his anointing by Elijah (*Dial.* 49), his healing of every sickness and disease (*Dial.* 49), his passion as the Just One (*Dial.* 98, 101-103, 105-107), his crucifixion (*Dial.* 98, 99, 104), his sacrifice as God's perfect paschal lamb (*Dial.* 13, 40, 72, 93), his resurrection and ascension (*Dial.* 36), his enthronement at God's right hand (*Dial.* 37), the disbelief of the Jews and the consequent destruction of Judea (*Dial.* 16), his substitution of circumcision with the living waters of baptism flowing from the 'good rock' (*Dial.* 114), and his current reign spreading out from Jerusalem through the apostles and the conversion of the nations (*Dial.* 24, 26, 109). These nations of believers were God's prophesied worshippers in Spirit and truth, cleansed of idolatry and all moral wickedness (*Dial.* 130, 131), and one day they would witness Christ's second coming in fulfilment of Daniel's prophecy (*Dial.* 31).

Justin believed that the Old Testament was also full of soteriological 'types' (τύποι) of Christ. Interpreters employing typology see historical and literal events, persons or objects of

---

169 Von Campenhausen, *The Fathers of the Greek Church*, p. 11. Osborn, "Justin's Response," p. 49, states that Justin's method of exegesis has its "clearest parallel … with Habakkuk commentary from Qumran and the Gospel according to St. Matthew." Shotwell, *Biblical Exegesis*, p. 46, observes, "It is highly probable that (Justin) was dependent upon his Christian precursors for some of his methods of allegorical interpretation. It is highly probable that Justin was influenced by his knowledge of Stoic allegorical interpretation … some of his methods of allegory could have come from Palestinian (Jewish) thought."

the past as foreshadowing greater realities in a subsequent time. So, for example, the Passover lamb (which was slain to achieve Israel's liberation from Egyptian bondage) was for Justin a forerunner of Jesus who, as the Lamb of God, was slain to liberate humanity from the bondage of the devil (*Dial.* 40). Justin saw other types of Jesus in the persons of Noah (*Dial.* 138), Jonah (*Dial.* 107, 108), Moses (*Dial.* 90, 91, 94, 97, 112), Joshua (*Dial.* 75, 90, 91, 106, 111, 112, 113, 115), the scapegoat (*Dial.* 40), and Rahab's scarlet rope (*Dial.* 111), while such 'symbols' (σύμβολον) as the twelve bells hanging from the high priest's robe prefigured "the twelve Apostles who relied upon the power of Christ, the Eternal Priest" (*Dial.* 42). As for the unleavened bread, such symbolised "that you do not commit the old deeds of the bad leaven" (*Dial.* 14), while the oblation of fine flour which was prescribed to be presented on behalf of those purified from leprosy was a type of the bread of the Eucharist, the sacrifice prescribed by Christ in fulfilment of the prophecy of Malachi (*Dial.* 41).

Considered together, these fulfilled prophecies and types constituted conclusive evidence for the veracity of Christianity ("the facts speak for themselves": *Dial.* 49 and 51), justifying the leaving behind of paganism and Jewish "hardness of heart" for the true God and "circumcision of the heart" (*Dial.* 113, 114). In cases of obscurity or doubt concerning a particular prophecy, Justin insisted on the reader's (or even his own) inability to understand the given passage (*Dial.* 65). Justin's allegorical interpretations were not set against other Jewish allegorical interpretations, but usually against a narrow literal interpretation of the text (for example, the interpretations that proposed Kings Solomon and Hezekiah as the persons fulfilling Psalms 23, 71 and 109 [*Dial.* 33, 34, 36, 84] and Isaiah 7 [*Dial.* 43, 83]). To see the fulfilment of Scripture in Christ, it was necessary to go beyond the literal reading (*Dial.* 112, 114), and for this the grace of God, or a "second circumcision," was necessary, a grace the Christians possessed (*Dial.* 58, 114, 119). Therefore, the only way to understand the prophets was to become a Christian, as inferred by the 'old man' in *Dial.* 7: "for no one can perceive or understand these truths unless he has been enlightened by God and his Christ."

The Jews, on the other hand, still failed to recognise the prophecies concerning Jesus, bringing down God's punishment and the desolation of their nation (*Dial.* 58, 113). According to Justin, there were so many prophecies fulfilled by Christ that the Jews needed to resort to mutilating their Scriptures, excising those passages that obviously referred to him. Justin also shows astonishment at the Jewish claim that no words of prophecy have yet been fulfilled (*Dial.* 110) and at their contentiousness in the face of obvious proof (*Dial.* 118), as well as their refusal to admit knowledge that damages their case (*Dial.* 125).

Justin believed that all his ends could be achieved by the appropriation of Old Testament prophecy through proving their fulfilment in Jesus of Nazareth. Another means employed by Justin to appropriate the Old Testament was his general theory of theophanies. According to Justin, every appearance of God to Abraham (*Dial.* 56), Jacob (*Dial.* 58), and Moses (*Dial.* 59, 60) was a manifestation of Christ. Though Justin struggled to explain how the Father and the Son were both God and yet distinct, his theory amounted to an original attempt to aggregate to Jesus an existence more ancient than any other venerable personality, whether pagan, Hebrew or Jewish, while combining the Old and New Testaments into one organic unity and depriving the former of its exclusive Jewishness.

Appropriateness of the argument

Justin's use of 'proof from prophecy' was entirely appropriate as regards his Christian audience as 'mainstream' Christians accepted the validity of the prophets and recognised the Old Testament as Scripture. There was therefore no need for Justin, as when writing his Apologies, to establish the antiquity or prophetic credentials of Moses and the Old Testament Scriptures, only to verify the fulfilment credentials of Jesus.

Arguments advanced by Justin in favour of Jesus' fulfilment of prophecy would have been eagerly received and regarded by those within 'the fold' as powerful ammunition to promote his messianic claims in apologetical encounters with Jews. Few Christians would have given critical attention to interpretations that proved that faith in Jesus was justified and that they were now central in God's plan. Moreover, the attitude to the Old Testament Justin imparted to the Christians was virtually identical to that of the Jews of his day (for it was from the Jews themselves that the Christians had taken their attitude to the Scriptures), namely, that it was an authoritative revelation, enabling the establishment of common grounds for debate between the two groups, as well as with Judaising Christians arguing for the retention of circumcision. Furthermore, by using Old Testament prophecy Justin could train his Christian audience to nuance their approach, arguing that they were not seeking to convert Jews or Judaisers to an alien worship, but rather to come to a correct view of their own religion, history and mission.

Justin's use of allegory and typology had the potential to provide further assistance. It introduced not only an element of future fulfilment but also undermined the narrow literal interpretation of the Torah, preparing the way for its 'abrogation' by Jesus. Justin could extensively employ such interpretative methods towards his Christian audience and through them to the Jews as the latter of the Alexandrian school were for a number of centuries engaged in extraordinary allegorisation, eventually influencing the Christians of the same city. Flowing from this, unattached Gentiles considering a choice between the two faiths would sooner or later become aware of this shared interest in symbolic interpretation and therefore feel the necessity to weigh up the different options on offer. In addition, every type Justin could find was an additional nail in Marcion's rejection of the Old Testament. Justin was free to employ symbolic interpretation with little restriction, as there was an absence of authority to declare how much of Scripture was open to non-literal interpretation and in what sense it could be otherwise interpreted.

However, though allegorical and typological interpretations of Scripture could make a prophecy's fulfilment in Jesus seem obvious to one already Christian, a sceptical or wavering eye would not see it so clearly as having been fulfilled by him. Barnard[170] labels a number of Justin's interpretations as "precarious in the extreme," while Osborn[171] speaks of his "recurring irrationality." Examples include the staffs of Moses and Aaron and all other staffs and trees of the Old Testament—for Justin all these were prefigurations of the cross of Christ (*Dial.* 86). Bokser[172] points out the unhistorical nature of Justin's typology, stating, "[e]vents separated by many centuries were treated as though they were contemporary." Shotwell[173] also complains of Justin's disregard for "the original context and meaning of the words [of prophecy]" by placing words on the lips of authors who lived more than a millennium before the occurrences to which

---

170 Barnard, *St. Justin Martyr*, p. 16.
171 Osborn, *Justin Martyr*, p. 107.
172 Bokser, "Justin Martyr and the Jews," p. 210.
173 Shotwell, *Biblical Exegesis*, p. 31.

they allude. Instead of being converted, many Jews would have simply rejected Justin's conclusions as biased interpretative gymnastics and left them with mistrust of allegorical exegesis as a method in general. Justin ran the very real risk of impressing no one except those who already accepted the premise that faith in Christ was the necessary foundation for understanding the Old Testament. Nevertheless, some of Justin's interpretations of the Old Testament may well have been persuasive if we are to trust the words put into the mouth of Trypho by Justin: "My friend … you have proved your point forcibly and with many arguments" (*Dial.* 63).

Concerning the theophanies, Justin's argument that they were always manifestations of Jesus would have gone down well with Christians seeking evidence of Christ in the Old Testament as well as his divinity. Furthermore, they would have amounted to another collective argument reinforcing the value of the Old Testament in opposition to Marcion's refusal to accept it as Scripture, as well as opposing his belief that the Gods of the Old and New Testaments were separate and opposing beings. However, the argument would have appeared confusing to those unattached Gentiles yet unfamiliar with the developing understandings of the Trinity, while Justin's awkward language referring to Jesus as "another God" (*Dial.* 56) would have further clouded matters as well as violently offended the strict monotheism of Judaism. The fact that Trypho was shocked at Justin's claim that it was Christ who spoke to Moses at the burning bush (*Dial.* 38, 40) evidences that Jewish sensitivities would have been greatly disturbed by an argument that seemed to banish the God of Abraham, Isaac and Jacob, hitherto active and living among his people, into the remote background, replaced by a divine Jesus who appeared to be no more than a man.

There are also problems with a number of Justin's Old

Testament citations. For Justin and Christians in general the Septuagint was the starting point for biblical exegesis and trusted as completely authentic and inspired (being the only text available to non-Jews).[174] However, there are a number of peculiarities in Justin's quotations from it. Osborn[175] lists them as follows: "He quotes freely, adapts the text to his own meaning, combines different quotations, attributes texts to wrong authors, [and] quotes the same text differently in different contexts … " Concerning the attribution of texts to wrong authors, Justin most probably imported these errors from second-century testimony-anthologies that were deviant vis-à-vis the original Septuagint text. It may also indicate that he used his source material in a haphazard manner, at times disregarding minutiae about text and authorship, not primarily concerned about which prophet spoke the prophecy so long as it had come to pass. Be that as it may, such use of the sacred text would have undermined Justin's apologetical endeavours, especially towards Jews and those Gentiles concerned enough to take time to closely examine his written claims. Furthermore, it was a time when Jewish resentment over Christian pre-empting of their sacred books was being manifested by an increasing distaste for the Septuagint. By doing the things he did, Justin would have reinforced Jewish suspicions of the Septuagint, suspicions that prompted Theodotion, Symmachus and Aquila to later produce their own translations of the Old Testament.

---

174 Barnard, *St. Justin Martyr*, p. 44. It was also in many instances the only Bible read out to large numbers of Greek-speaking Jews throughout the Diaspora.
175 Osborn, *Justin Martyr*, p. 113.

The Argument from Miracles

Purpose: To convert unattached Gentiles, fortify Christians

Similarly to pagans, the Jews believed that from time to time there appeared men who were specially gifted with the power to perform miracles: Moses (thirteenth century BC), Elijah and Elisha (ninth century BC) are some of the better known examples. Both pagans and Jews also generally viewed miracles in terms of power authenticating the claims of the wonder-worker. In his Apologies, Justin's protreptic sought to employ Jesus' miracles to effect a change in judicial policy and win pagan converts; in *Dialogue* it was to establish and reinforce the latter's messianic credentials to win unattached Gentiles and fortify existing Christians.

In a comment that reflected specific Jewish and Christian belief Justin wrote of the prophets as "worthy of belief because of the miracles which they performed, for they exalted God, the Father and Creator of all things" (*Dial.* 7). What then of the Messiah? Did those Jews who still awaited his coming expect the performance of miracles as a condition for acceptance? Certainly those Jews who understood Isaiah 35:5-6 as messianic would have. It seemed that Justin was aware of this and so endeavoured to establish Jesus' fulfilment of this specific piece of scripture in the following terms:

> The fountain of living water which gushed forth from God upon a land devoid of the knowledge of God (that is, the land of the Gentiles) was our Christ, who made his appearance on earth in the midst of your people, and healed those who from birth were blind and deaf and lame. He cured them by his word, causing them to walk, to hear, and to

see. By restoring the dead to life, he compelled the men of that day to recognise him. Yet, though they witnessed these miraculous deeds with their own eyes, they attributed them to magical art; indeed, they dared to call him a magician who misled the people. But he performed these deeds to convince his future followers (*Dial.* 69).

The above paragraph is the most extensive reference made by Justin in *Dialogue* concerning the miracles of Jesus and touches on all the key issues relating to the argument: the different types of miracles Jesus performed; the compelling power of his miracles before his contemporary audience, especially those of resuscitation; the intention to convince future believers; and the accusation by the Jews that Jesus was a deceiver of the people who performed deeds that were attributable to magic.

In addition to this last accusation, Justin displayed an awareness of other attacks commonly raised against the miracles of Jesus, namely: (i) that diabolical counterfeits were often indistinguishable from divine wonders (*Dial.* 69); and (ii) that pagan miracle accounts were similar to and preceded those of Christ, rendering the latter unoriginal (*Dial.* 69).

There was also the problem that miracles normally carry conviction only with actual eyewitnesses of the alleged phenomena. Justin sought to pre-empt this by extending his appeal to the gifts received by neophytes, including "the spirit of wisdom, … counsel, … fortitude, … healing, … foreknowledge, … teaching, and the fear of God" (*Dial.* 39). As with his Apologies (*2 Apol.* 6), Justin also referred to exorcisms carried out in the name of Jesus by contemporary Christians: "We call him our Helper and Redeemer, by the power at whose name even the demons shudder; even to this day are overcome by us when we exorcise them in the name of Jesus Christ, who was crucified under Pontius Pilate, the Governor of Judea"

(*Dial.* 30; cf. *Dial.* 76, 111, 121). On the other hand, exorcisms performed by Jews in the name of others (whether kings, just men, prophets or patriarchs) were powerless to subdue the demons, while certain Jews adjured demons "by employing the magical art of the Gentiles, using fumigations and amulets" (*Dial.* 85).

Appropriateness of the argument

Miracles as an argument in favour of Jesus' messianic credentials was one that Justin was compelled to proffer considering the well-known prophecy in Isaiah 35:5-6. Justin quoted this verse fully in *Dialogue* 69 knowing that discussion relating to it would inevitably arise in any contact with prospective converts, whether Jewish or unattached Gentile. Solid evidence that Jesus performed miracles needed to be adduced and of a kind to surpass the stories of miracle-working Jewish rabbis that were widely circulated during the first and second centuries AD. Examples of the latter included Honi the Circle Drawer (+AD 65), Hanina ben Dosa (c. AD 70-100) and Eliezer ben Hyrcanus (end of first century AD) who were said to have performed miracles (including rainmaking, healings, and surviving snakebite) to emphasise teachings and reinforce doctrinal decisions.

The accusation that Christ was "a magician who misled the people" was the standard Jewish-rabbinical response[176] to

---

176 According to Jacob Neusner, *Messiah in Context: Israel's History and Destiny in Formative Judaism, Part Two: Teleology*, Fortress Press, Philadelphia, 1984, p. 63, "A kind of 'anti-Gospel,' narrating nasty stories about Jesus, could have been constructed; later on it was. Along these same lines, a systematic narrative of several rabbis' opposition to Jesus and his teachings, pursuing lines of consistent discourse, surely could have emerged even from the mere stringing together of tales." However, while Justin (and later Origen) ascribed rabbinic thoughts to the Jews in general rabbinic literature was not entirely representative of early Jewish attitudes toward Christianity, as "the majority of Jews with whom Christians interacted probably did not feel bound by rabbinic teaching" (Wilson, *Related Strangers*, p. 194).

the claimed miracles of Jesus and struck deeply at his moral character.[177] According to the Law of Moses, magic was prohibited and punishable by death (Lev. 19:26; Deut. 18:10; Exod. 22:18). Specific examples of such accusations contained in rabbinic writings include:

> On the eve of the Passover they hung Jeshu. And the crier went forth before him forty days, saying, "He goes forth to be stoned because he has practised magic and deceived and led Israel astray. Anyone who knows anything in his favour let him come and declare concerning him." And they found nothing in his favour. And they hung him on the eve of Passover.[178]

> It is tradition that Rabbi Eliezer said to the sages, "Did not Ben Stada bring spells from Egypt in a cut which was upon his flesh?" They said to him, "He was a fool, and they do not base a proof upon a fool." Ben Stada is Ben Pandira.[179]

> And a teacher has said, "Jesus the Nazarene practised magic and led astray and deceived Israel."[180]

---

177 There were also attacks disputing Jesus' birth, that his mother was a poor adulteress and his father a soldier named Pandera (or Pantera): Babylonian Talmud tractate, Sanhedrin 67a.

178 Babylonian Talmud tractate, Sanhedrin 43a. Wilson, *Related Strangers*, p. 185, states that this passage "is one of the clearest references to Jesus in rabbinic tradition, and for that reason was deleted in some manuscripts. Like most such material it is a mixture of firm reference and garbled detail."

179 Babylonian Talmud tractate, Sanhedrin 104b.

180 Babylonian Talmud tractate, Sanhedrin 107b. It is often suggested that these rabbinic traditions are too confused and legendary to be of any real historic value. However, even if such were true, this does not entirely negate their value. If we accept the view of Wilson, *Related Strangers*, p. 186, a distinction can be made "between the accusation itself and its confused and legendary framework, and we cannot assume that something added to the Babylonian Talmud had no prior life in Jewish communal tradition."

Justin and others provide evidence that the accusations of magic and deception levelled against Jesus had already spread far and wide by the second half of the second century. Justin alleged that the Jews were busy sending emissaries throughout the world to counter Christianity as a godless and lawless sect founded by a deceiver (*Dial.* 17, 108). He may himself have heard the charges against Jesus directly from Jews familiar with rabbinic literature for he repeated precisely in substance the rabbinic allegation in his own native Greek. A few decades later Celsus admitted that his knowledge of Jesus as a magician who had learnt his craft in Egypt came from a Jewish informant.[181] That being the case, it is most likely that unattached Gentiles such as Marcus Pompeius considering the respective claims of Christianity and Judaism would have encountered the same allegations (and perhaps from both pagan and Jewish sources) and existing Jews engaged in debate with Christians fully imbued with them. Hence, there was a clear need for Justin to advance appropriate arguments in rebuttal.

The arguments Justin advanced inevitably were similar to those put forward in his Apologies. As when addressing the emperors, Justin hinted in *Dialogue* that he was conscious of the connection between works of magic and magical paraphernalia, spells and incantations, and therefore the consequent need to highlight the lack of such matter in Jesus' wonders. According to Mair[182], "[i]f the resolution of the difficulty is sought through the manipulation of forces, the activity is primarily magical. If aid is sought through communication with beings, then the

---

181 Origen, *Against Celsus* 1.28.38. There is no reason to doubt Celsus' claim that he was following a Jewish source, thereby placing the anti-Christian tradition c. AD 170. Celsus thus provides evidence that the rabbinic writings, though admittedly confused and legendary, assimilated accusations that were undoubtedly circulating in the second century.

182 L. P. Mair, *An Introduction to Social Anthropology*, Clarendon Press, Oxford, 1965, p. 229.

activity is primarily religious." Justin attempted to shift focus to the latter in two ways, first, by stating that Jesus cured the blind, deaf, and lame solely "by his word" (*Dial.* 69) and, second, by repeating the claim that contemporary Christians carried out exorcisms "in the name of Jesus Christ" (*Dial.* 30, 76, 111, 121). Both claims had the potential benefit of impressing the reader that, unlike pagan magicians or Jewish miracle-workers, Jesus did not include material objects or prayer in his actions but spoke simple commands to effect them through a power that was inherently his own.

However, such evidence could easily have been contested by any Gentile or Jew aware of Jesus' use of automatically effective techniques considered as hallmarks of magic, including touch (Matt. 20:34; Mark 7:33; Luke 22:51), sighs (Mark 7:34), and saliva (Mark 7:33; 8:23; John 9:6). Justin ought to have mentioned miracles involving these particular techniques by way of pre-emption, providing the following explanations: (i) hands: there existed no evidence that Jesus regarded his hands as magical instruments or that he protected them with amulets, a usual practice of magicians; (ii) sighs: these were a simple expression of emotion, as natural to cult as to magic; (iii) saliva: Jesus healed with and without saliva, the majority being without, and that use of saliva was simply an enhanced form of touch; and (iv) openness: Jesus always performed his cures openly and at a distance, allowing those around him to clearly hear his words and observe his actions.

Regarding the allegation that Jesus' miracles were diabolical counterfeits, Justin simply 'turned-the-tables' with a forensic attack against alleged pagan miracle accounts: "he who is called the Devil counterfeited [signs] in the fictions circulated among the Greeks (just as he accomplished them through the Egyptian magicians and the false prophets in the days of Elijah)" (*Dial.* 69). This was also the case particularly with Bacchus, Hercules, and Asclepius, the latter especially elevated by the devil as a raiser of the dead and healer of all diseases in imitation of the prophecies about Christ (*Dial.* 69). However, Justin could have done more to refute this accusation by providing a specific rebuttal similar to Origen's[183] given in the mid-third century, which focused on motive:

> [I]n fact no sorcerer uses his tricks to call spectators to moral reformation; nor does he educate by the fear of God people who were astounded by what they saw, nor does he attempt to persuade the onlookers to live as men who will be judged by God. Sorcerers do none of those things, since they have neither the ability nor even the will to do so.

Justin could also have done more by appealing to Jesus' moral character (*ethos*): the holiness of Christ's life and those of his followers; that the extraordinary phenomena were usually acts of healing and kindness for the poor and afflicted; the absence of mercenary motives; the good and long-term effects of Jesus' healings and exorcisms; and the complete lack of immorality and squalid details normally associated with pagan wonders.

As mentioned also, the miracles of Jesus were vulnerable to the accusation that they were simply ordinary compared to stories of the miraculous found in ancient pagan literature, or more to the point were directly plagiarised from earlier pagan writings. Unattached Gentiles such as Marcus Pompeius would undoubtedly have been familiar with at least some of the alleged exploits of the ancient gods and heroes. For example, Bacchus and Hercules, who were both said to have resurrected and ascended into heaven, and Asclepius was known for "raising the dead to life and curing all diseases" (*Dial.* 69). We read of another resurrection account in the life of the Egyptian god-king Osiris (c. 3000 BC) and of Romulus appearing to his

---

183 Origen, *Against Celsus* 1.68.

followers after his bodily ascension into heaven (eighth century BC).

In response, Justin could have exposed the charges of plagiarism as baseless by simply highlighting that similarity does not of itself amount to evidence of reliance. Justin, however, did not demand the production of such evidence. Instead, he chose to reverse the charge of plagiarism against the Gentiles. The prophecies concerning the miracles of Christ in fact preceded the Greek and Romans. Having knowledge of these prophecies, the devil inspired imitations to pre-empt the coming of Christ. Justin hoped that such a line of argument would have given his audience the same confidence he himself possessed: "Rest assured, then, Trypho … he who is called the Devil counterfeited [signs] in the fictions circulated among the Greeks (just as he accomplished them through the Egyptian magicians and the false prophets in the days of Elijah) … ought I not conclude that the Scriptural passage that speaks of Christ, strong as a giant to run his course, was similarly imitated?" (*Dial.* 69). Justin thus simultaneously exposed the origin of alleged pagan miracles and undermined the credibility of the pagan gods through a forensic strategy that highlighted the latter's impotence and subjugation to the demons.

By charging that Jewish exorcists were guilty of "employing the magical art of the Gentiles, using fumigations and amulets" (*Dial.* 85) Justin once more employed 'turning-of-the-tables' rhetoric. By reversing such a charge he hoped to expose the Jews to hypocrisy and so undermine their line of attack that Jesus was a magician and deceiver. However, Justin made his counter-charge in a one-off sentence and failed to provide any supporting evidence such as the names of particular Jewish exorcists or miracle accounts mentioning the use of suspect substances. Furthermore, Justin's mention of the failure of contemporary Jewish exorcists to cast out demons in the name of "kings, just men, prophets, or patriarchs" aimed to emphasise the now impotent state of Judaism, a matter Justin could have reinforced by highlighting that the number of cures mentioned in accounts of Jewish miracle-workers were nowhere near the number performed by Jesus.[184]

As was the case when writing to the emperors, it was necessary to avoid the entanglement of trying to prove the integrity of the apostolic witnesses. By pressing instead claims of contemporary Christian miracles of healing and exorcism, Justin pursued the only path that could provide the necessary objective and demonstrable evidence. To quote once again the words of Remus, "[t]he relation between 'then' and 'now' was reciprocal and mutually reinforcing: the extraordinary happenings in the Jesus story made extraordinary happenings in the present seem plausible, and vice versa."[185] There was also a clear implication: the divine authority originally held by the Jews was now in the hands of those who currently proclaim the name of Jesus and carry forward his Gospel throughout the world.

The Argument from True Israel

Purpose: To convert unattached Gentiles, fortify Christians, combat Judaising Christians, counter Marcionism

Justin's *adversus Iudaeos* apologetic asserted Christianity's superiority over Judaism as the fullness and completion of what had been only partial before. Moses had only led the Hebrews to the Holy Land and a temporary inheritance. Those who confessed Jesus as the fulfilment of the Scriptures and as the

---

184 M. Smith, *Tannaitic Parallels to the Gospels*, Society of Biblical Literature, Philadelphia, 1951, pp. 81-84.
185 Remus, *Pagan-Christian Conflict*, p. 152.

new law and lawgiver were now part of God's 'true Israel' (*Dial.* 11, 12, 14, 135), superseding the Israel of the Old Testament, and destined to inherit an eternal portion (*Dial.* 113): "We have been led to God through this crucified Christ, and we are the true spiritual Israel, and the descendents of Judah, Jacob, Isaac and Abraham" (*Dial.* 11).[186] This was Justin's "militant supersessionism," which asserted that Christianity had inherited Israel's spiritual legacy and supplanted its original recipient. Israel was no longer God's ambassador to the nations, but a perverse nation blind-folded and led astray by her leaders and teachers (*Dial.* 9, 38, 48), and rejected due to its hard-heartedness (*Dial.* 27, 53).[187] As Justin declared: "Thus, God promised a religious and righteous nation of like faith, and a delight to the Father; but it is not you, in whom there is not faith" (*Dial.* 119). They were not to be saved, especially those Jews who anathematised in their synagogues those who accepted Jesus as the Christ (*Dial.* 25, 26, 47). Christians were now in Israel's stead, the true people of God (*Dial.* 110), the high-priestly race (*Dial.* 116), and were to receive the inheritance in the holy city (*Dial.* 26). While the true Israel was already spreading to the ends of the earth through its universal missionary mandate, the Israel of old had been reduced to enacting reactionary communal measures against Christians (*Dial.* 31, 38, 112, 133), and sending forth

---

186 Concerning the belief that the Christian Church is the true Israel, Osborn, *Justin Martyr*, pp. 171 and 176, states, "Justin is the chief source for knowledge of this development … The idea of a true Israel is definitive for the *Dialogue*, occurring at the beginning of the work and dominating the final chapters." Daniel Boyarin, "Justin Martyr Invents Judaism," *Church History* 70 (2001) pp. 427-461 at p. 435, states "the claim to be *Verus Israel* … [was] … first attested in Justin but surely not originated by him."

187 Jewish reasons for opposing Christianity included, *inter alia*, that it was a "godless and lawless heresy" (αἱρεσίς τις αθεος καὶ ανομος) that worshipped a man instead of God (*Dial.* 8). Christians may have cited the Old Testament, but they had abandoned the Law and the prophets, and in their place substituted a Gospel that made demands that were impossible to keep (*Dial.* 10), while, at the same time, their lives were no different from those of the Gentiles (*Dial.* 10).

anti-Christian emissaries throughout the world (*Dial.* 17).[188]

Justin supported his accusations against the Jewish nation by quoting from Jewish Scripture. He believed that the key to understanding the Old Testament was faith in Christ. The rejection of Christ was the principal reason why the Jews did not understand the very Scriptures they treasured as their own: "Aren't you acquainted with them, Trypho? You should be, for they are contained in your Scriptures, or rather not yours, but ours. For we believe and obey them, whereas you, when you read them, do not grasp their spirit" (*Dial.* 29). It was the recognition of Jesus as the fulfilment of Old Testament Scripture that also passed 'ownership' of the latter to the Christians. He asserted that the Jews, in support of their 'stubborn resistance,' rejected the Septuagint translation, falsified and twisted the meaning of Scripture, and omitted messianic prophecies that clearly referred to Jesus (*Dial.* 71-73, 84). Isaiah himself foretold the apostasy of Israel (*Dial.* 133). Circumcision was a sign that indicated the future estrangement of the Jews, symbolising how God would sever them from the other nations and single them out for punishment for failing to believe (*Dial.* 16, 23, 92).[189]

Justin added to these assertions by arguing that the Law of Moses had been superseded, replaced by the universal, perfect and eternal law of Jesus Christ (*Dial.* 11, 12, 24, 67, 100). Justin cited Isaiah and Jeremiah, claiming that they respectively foretold a new law and a new covenant for the Gentiles (*Dial.* 11-12). In

---

188 There continues to be much controversy over the accuracy of Justin's references to Jewish anti-Christian measures; however, Horbury, *Jews and Christians in Contact and Controversy*, p. 156, concedes that "… although defective reporting is inevitable in the circumstances, [Justin] will have had some good sources and some personal knowledge."

189 Justin may have been inspired with such a symbolic explanation of the purpose of circumcision by a belief that the Romans, after legally excluding all Jews from Jerusalem after the Bar Cochba revolt of AD 132-135, conducted physical searches at the entrance of the city to identify and punish any Jews who attempted to flaunt the prohibition: Rokéah, *Justin Martyr and the Jews*, p. 57.

Justin's view, it was necessary to distinguish between the ritual and moral precepts of the Law. Only the moral demands of the Law were eternally binding as they were founded in the nature of God himself (*Dial.* 23). The ceremonial demands of the Law were more of a reproach imposed upon the Hebrew peoples for their hardness of heart and worship of the golden calf (*Dial.* 18, 45). Circumcision, fasts, sabbaths, new moons, sacrifices, and the Temple were only ordained to curtail the innate tendency of the Jews towards sin and idolatry (*Dial.* 19, 22, 27, 46, 67, 92). Christians, however, practised a second 'circumcision of the heart' rather than the flesh (*Dial.* 12, 19, 113, 114), enjoyed a continual sabbath not limited to a single day (*Dial.* 12), abstained through a true fast involving rejection of "every band of wickedness" (*Dial.* 15), and cleansed themselves in a true bathing not of the body but of the soul (*Dial.* 29). That Adam, Abel, Enoch, Melchizedeck, and Abraham were justified in the eyes of God without physical circumcision was proof enough for Justin that "circumcision is not essential for all men, but only for the Jews" (*Dial.* 19, 23, 27, 28). Justification depended, not on being of the seed of Abraham, but on imitating his faith in God, which meant for Christians having faith in Christ, as well as moral integrity, repentance and obedience (*Dial.* 23).[190] The coming of Christ was not only the continuation but also the climax of God's plan to restore humanity to his friendship. Christ was the new Adam; Mary was the new Eve (*Dial.* 100).

Justin believed that God had punished the Jews for their rejection of Christ. He saw the destruction of Jerusalem and its Temple as a just retribution for their unbelief (*Dial.* 92, 110). There were no more sacrifices, kings or prophets for the Jews,

---

190 In his summary, Rokéah, *Justin Martyr and the Jews*, p. 130, concludes: "One might say that Justin follows Paul faithfully in presenting the Torah as a negative work that lost all its relevance after the advent of Jesus … Following Paul, Justin argues that it is not the Torah that leads to righteousness, but faith, as proved by the fact that Abraham acquired righteousness while still uncircumcised."

and their land was made waste, while the Gentiles converted to Christ and awaited his second coming (*Dial.* 52). The prophetic gifts were transferred from the Jews to the Christians (*Dial.* 82); and it was the Gentiles who, as predicted by the prophet Malachi, now offered the only pleasing sacrifices to God (*Dial.* 13, 15, 28, 41, 115). However, even the destruction of Jerusalem had not led to Israel's repentance; rather, it had intensified her hostility.

While there was hope for a remnant of the Jews to be saved (*Dial.* 32, 55), for the hard-hearted only prayer was possible (*Dial.* 133); and Justin hoped for and expected the eventual repentance of Israel (*Dial.* 108).

Appropriateness of the argument

Justin's claim that Christians were now "Israel, the true children of Abraham and the true children of God" (*Dial.* 11, 123) was meant as a protreptic argument to move Trypho and his companions to embrace Christianity, but was met instead with stunned silence, anger and rowdiness (*Dial.* 122-124). This was not surprising considering the uncompromising nature of Justin's rhetoric, which suggested not only a 'takeover' of language and imagery normally used by the Jews to describe themselves but also a discontinuity and dialectic between Judaism and Christianity (*Dial.* 12, 26, 110, 116, 130, 135).

Like the Apostle Paul, Justin considered that in Christ he had become a fulfilled son of Israel and yearned that all Jews saw, trusted and accepted what he did—that Jesus was the long-awaited Messiah and new law giver (*Dial.* 11). This was not an unreasonable expectation for a Christian, for it follows logically that if Jesus was the one who fulfilled the Old Testament messianic prophecies then Christianity must consequently be the fulfilment and completion of Judaism. It gave important self-definition to the Christian community for his Christian readers and presented Christianity as a clear and solid alternative for unattached Gentiles.

Should Justin, however, have modified his militant supersessionism so as not to offend Jewish sensitivities? Supersessionism implies a 'doing away with' in the manner of, for example, a caterpillar that sheds its cocoon upon becoming a butterfly. It is arguable that in order to avoid inciting hostility and tension Justin should have proposed more moderate positions (similar to those of St Paul in Romans 11:1-2, 28-31), namely, that the Old Covenant was brought to fruition, not superseded, by the New, that Jesus as Messiah completed and crowned, not discarded, the Mosaic religion, and that the Law was not done away with but rather fulfilled, its understanding perfected more than changed. Furthermore, Justin could have asserted that the blessing of nature promised to "the seed of Abraham" had now matured into the "blessing by choice" for both Jew and non-Jew, thereby placing Jews and Gentiles on the same footing. By adopting such arguments, Justin's Christian readers in their contacts with Jews would have avoided the type of rancour that inevitably renders all missionary efforts fruitless.

May the same be said of Justin's anti-Jewish generalisations and vituperative comments? Horner[191] states that, "sometimes it is the thick end of unbridled accusation and harsh polemic." Examples of such are found in *Dial.* 32, 39, 44, 55, 64, 68, 92, 110, 120, 134. Of these, perhaps the most pungent is contained in *Dial.* 120:

> ... others, also children of Abraham, would be like the sand on the sea-shore, which, though vast and extensive, is barren and fruitless, not bearing any fruit at all, but only drinking up the water of the sea. Of this a great part of your people is guilty, for you

---

191 Horner, "Justin's Mission to the Jews," p. 42.

all imbibe bitter and godless doctrines, while you
spurn the word of God.

Rajak[192] asserts that "the largest part of the *Dialogue*" is
characterised by this vituperative spirit, though it is "punctuated
by moments of genuine interaction."[193] If Justin ever envisaged
that his arguments would reach the ears of Jews then the
following question needs to be asked: is it possible that any Jews
would have been attracted by arguments couched in insensitive,
angry, or even offensive language? The most probable answer
is "no." Yet Justin's *Dialogue* exhibited these aspects before his
Gentile and Christian readers as part and parcel of his suggested
apologetic. Perhaps as *Dialogue* was written against the Jews but
not to them then Justin's harsh language was understandable,
serving to highlight the errors of the Jews in the minds of
Gentiles and Christians who would be the judges of such
arguments. However, why would Justin include an invitation for
Trypho to convert at the end of *Dialogue* unless he believed that
his audience should likewise seek the conversion of Jews? This
is significant, for while Justin was carried away by enthusiasm
and emotion in his efforts to assert his militant super-sessionism
he nevertheless knew what was the best way to present his
arguments and expressed it well in *Dial.* 79: "Desiring to retain
his attention, I answered in much milder language."

Nevertheless, are such expectations appropriate from the
point of view of second century apologetic discourse? We must
avoid the temptation of judging Justin according to religious
sensibilities characteristic of modern-day pluralistic societies.
It must be remembered that it was Trypho himself who first

---

192 Rajak, "Talking at Trypho," p. 60.
193 Rajak, "Talking at Trypho," p. 61. This is evidenced by the friendly tone directed
to Trypho in *Dial.* 87, 88, 89, 90 and 96 as he tried to draw him into conversion-
style conversation. On one occasion Justin also consciously determined to use milder
language towards Trypho (*Dial.* 79), and on another expressed genuine pity towards
him and Jews in general (*Dial.* 37).

excluded Christians from salvation and dismissed Jesus as a deceiver and of no reputation (*Dial.* 9) when learning of Justin's conversion from Platonism. In such a context Justin's strong and equally exclusive response would not have come as a surprise or shocked Trypho and his companions. The same may be said for most other Jews, some of who would have been familiar with the strong language employed in that distinctive form of Jewish literature known as pesher, which was characteristic of the Qumran community, for example. Furthermore, threats were typical of ancient protreptic discourses, including those with educational and missionary intentions, while vituperative language played an important role in didactic discourses. Together with the fact that counter-accusations were considered a valid strategy in forensic rhetoric it is arguable that Justin's writings were emblematic of second century works and hence no more offensive than most other religious writings of antiquity.

Justin's division of the Law into two categories (ethical commands and ritual prescriptions) was both logical and reasonable, serving as it did his purposes for writing: unattached Gentiles could perceive what was essential and what was not, and why; Gentile Christians could more effectively resist the arguments of Judaising Christians wishing to foist law-keeping upon them; Christians could confidently continue in their reverence yet non-observance of the Law in opposition to the respective claims of the Marcionites and Jews.

However, Justin's reasons for his division lead to some serious difficulties. Justin believed that the ethical prescriptions remained for Jews and Gentiles for they "were given for the worship of God and the practice of virtue" (*Dial.* 44); however, in his view the ritual prescriptions were now obsolete for Gentiles as they were only imposed on the Jews due to "the hardness of [their] hearts" (*Dial.* 44). Such an opinion transformed the long-held Jewish view that the Law and its precepts were a positive gift signifying the election of Israel into evidence of that nation's perversity. God, therefore, only imposed the precepts as a curative or, as in the case of circumcision (*Dial.* 23, 92), a punitive measure.

Justin's eagerness to render circumcision obsolete resulted in his developing an argument that not only contradicted Genesis 17 but also unduly blackened the reputation of the Jews as a nation from the beginning. Whether Justin was intending to exploit prophetic internal criticism of circumcision is uncertain. Nevertheless, it was probably the weakest part of his whole *Dialogue*. Genesis clearly speaks of circumcision as "a sign of the covenant between me and you" (17:11). Justin deliberately omitted the words "of the covenant" when quoting Genesis 17:11 in *Dial.* 23. Circumcision was in reality a sign of union and blessing, not a sign of curse. If circumcision made the Jews distinct it was to facilitate better their preparation as the messianic people through which the other nations would be blessed, not to prepare them in advance for punishment for rejecting the Messiah. Another weakness of this argument lay in its presupposing that circumcision was purely a Jewish phenomenon when in fact Justin and the Jews knew from reading Jeremiah that it was practised also by various pagan nations (*Dial.* 28).[194]

Justin would have done much better to emphasise the pedagogic nature of the Law, that it was given to prepare the descendants of Abraham and that there were always Jews throughout the intervening centuries who were its worthy and faithful observers. Unquestionably, the Law possessed a negative side as a response to Jewish unbelief and hardheartedness, but it also had a positive side that led them to repentance

---

194 Justin, *Dial.* 28: "For, behold, the days come, says the Lord, and I will visit upon every one that has their foreskin circumcised; upon Egypt, and Judah, and Edom, and upon the children of Moab."

and obedience. Such an argument would also have countered Marcionism by refuting any suggestion that the God of the Old Testament acted inconsistently with the God of the New, or that different Gods were responsible for the different demands made at different times. At the same time, Justin could still have maintained that with the coming of Jesus as Messiah the ceremonial precepts were fulfilled and dissolved in him, leaving only the ethical commands standing.

Justin's claim that the Scriptures (i.e., the Old Testament) were "rather not yours, but ours … For we believe and obey them" (*Dial.* 29) was a dramatic assertion that aimed to clearly highlight a paramount difference between Christianity and Judaism for prospective Gentile converts. For Gentiles who valued the Old Testament it was a claim that certainly would have captured their attention and compelled an examination of Justin's supporting evidence. If adequately supported, it had the potential to be the decisive argument. For those who were already Christian, Justin's supporting scriptural exegesis would have been welcomed as providing invaluable knowledge of the Old Testament and how it related to Christ. At the same time, it would have reinforced the value of the Old Testament as relevant and authentic Scripture for Christians in the face of Marcionite rejection.

Nonetheless, such a claim received via general apologetical encounters with Christians would have struck at the heart of any practising Jew, even those as hellenised as Trypho and his companions. It would have been regarded as an attempt to disinherit them of what they held to be most sacred, or to steal it outright. To apply a modern analogy, it would be akin to when the Europeans entered and occupied Australia claiming it to be 'empty land' (*terra nullius*), ignoring the pre-existing local Aboriginal peoples. The same could be said for Justin's accusation that the Jews were guilty of certain expurgations from the Septuagint text that clearly referred to Jesus. It was a grave charge that required direct evidence as proof. Yet, no certain evidence of such tampering exists and in the case of one example put forward by Justin—Jer. 9:19—all Greek and Hebrew Mss retain it.[195]

If individual Jews themselves received a copy of Justin's *Dialogue*, they would have regarded his claim to the Scriptures on behalf of Christianity as spurious for other reasons. Justin quoted from the Greek Septuagint version at a time when the Jews were questioning the authenticity and accuracy of texts used from it to establish the messianic credentials of Jesus. The copy of the Septuagint Justin used certainly contained corruptions, revisions, and additions in comparison with the Hebrew text.[196] As noted earlier, Justin also quoted verses from the Pentateuch, the Prophets and the Hagiographa ignoring their historical, political and social context and some of his typological and other interpretations vexed common sense. Failure by Justin to first establish his credentials to interpret Scripture would have exposed his higher claim to ownership to serious challenge.

Justin's apologetic would have been more persuasive if he did not so adamantly deny Jewish ownership of the Scriptures but rather recognised the Jews as their original custodians and guardians and as the people who successfully preserved them through the various historical phases of desolation, exile, and foreign domination. Instead of arguing about 'ownership' of Scripture, Justin should have confined himself to the question of its interpretation. Nor should Justin have accused the Jews of not believing in the Scriptures because of their rejection of Jesus; rather, he should have highlighted that they at least accepted as authentic Scripture those verses Christians saw as

---

195 L. W. Barnard, "The Old Testament and Judaism in the Writings of Justin Martyr," *Vetus Testamentum* 14 (1964), pp. 395-406 at p. 400.
196 Rokéah, *Justin Martyr and the Jews*, p. 126.

verifying Jesus' claims to messiahship. Justin would then have established the necessary groundwork into which aspects of the life of Jesus could be presented as light revealing a new and deeper understanding of Scripture.

The belief that the Jews were an apostate people punished by God for their rejection of Christ was an oft-repeated theme not only in the writings of Justin but of other early Christian writers as well. Justin's attacks echoed much of the past prophetic criticism of Jewish religious life. The Jews, who read the same Scriptures as the Christians yet rejected Jesus, would have appeared to many Christians as stubborn if not rebellious. This view would have been entrenched by the New Testament, which depicted them as the wicked tenants who killed the son of the vineyard owner (Matt. 21:33-46) or even as sons of the devil (John 8:39-59). Justin's portrayal of the Jews would have been received and accepted by existing Christians as consistent with and reinforcing these images. These images, constituting an "us versus them" paradigm, were fundamental to the process of Christian self-definition. To unattached Gentiles, they enhanced the starkness of the choice between Christianity and Judaism. Justin could portray Christianity as a much more attractive proposition, one to which Gentiles everywhere were already flocking and waiting in hope for the triumphal return of their King (*Dial.* 52). In contrast, pointing out the destruction of Jerusalem and its Temple, the despoliation of Judea, and the subsequent mass diaspora of the Jews would undoubtedly have devalued the appeal of Judaism.

However, Justin went further by proposing that the Hebrews from the time of Abraham and later the Jews were constantly in rebellion against God and deserving of punishment. A succession of quotes from the Law and the prophets were adduced to illustrate a constant history of infidelity, immorality and rejection of God's mercy culminating in the crucifixion of

Christ (e.g., *Dial.* 12, 46). Though Justin did not believe that all Jews were doomed because of their Jewishness he was of the opinion that only a small minority would be part of the 'remnant' group, a group Justin invited Trypho to join (*Dial.* 32, 55, 142). Justin's purpose was to prepare his audience to accept the suggestion that God had justly replaced the Jews with a new people prepared to keep his covenants. Such a 'pro-Christian' interpretation of history had the potential to achieve two objectives: (i) to distance Christians from the Jews while at the same time claim continuity with God's designs; and (ii) to rebut the Marcionite notion that the God of the Old Testament was God of the Jews only, who was separate from and inferior to the God of the Christians.

Justin was correct in his pointing out that the history of the Hebrews/Jews vis-à-vis God was not always a happy one. Stanton[197] terms it as the Sin-Exile-Return (S-E-R) pattern. Two examples among many are found in Exod. 32:7-14 (the grumbling and idolatrous Jews in the desert) and 1 Kgs 18 (the drought over the land of Israel). Though reflecting the spirit of prophetic criticism, Justin failed to emphasise that in all instances of past Hebrew/Jewish infidelity there always remained faithful Hebrews/Jews through which God continued to work. Justin especially needed to recognise such fidelity, as, unlike the prophets, his critique was external rather than internal and hence prone to the accusation of bias. Justin's non-recognition of this historical remnant made it more convenient for him to construct his 'pro-Christian' history but it did severe injustice to both the name and history of the Hebrew/Jewish people. It was an historical construction many uneducated Christians or neophytes would have adopted without question and if they passed it on in their own encounters with Jews it would have

---

197 Stanton, G. N., "Aspects of Early Christian-Jewish Polemic and Apologetic," *New Testament Studies* 31 (1985), pp. 377-392 at 385 ff.

been easily recognised as deliberately one-eyed and selective, thereby contributing nothing but damage to the Christian argument.

Even from a purely Christian perspective Justin's apologetic was remiss, failing to take into account the Apostle Paul who holds an eschatological hope for a Jewish remnant in his epistle to the Romans.[198] According to St Paul, the New Covenant, which brought fruition to the Old Covenant, will itself be brought to fruition with the eventual embracing of Jesus by the Jews before the end of time. A greater recognition and emphasis of this 'end times' corporate conversion (in contrast to just the conversion of a remnant of individuals from time to time) by Justin and other Christian apologists would have pre-empted and forestalled the later demonisation of the Jewish people that occurred at certain later times in certain places. Instead, Justin lost sight of the hope of salvation for Israel and, in the words of Skarsaune[199], "deteriorate[d] into a self-righteous declaration that 'you Jews' have an intrinsic quality of disbelief, while 'we Gentiles' have a greater willingness to belief." Justin falls into the attitude against which Paul so urgently warns in Rom. 11:17-22.

---

198 "*I ask, then, has God rejected his people? By no means!* I myself am an Israelite, a descendant of Abraham, a member of the tribe of Benjamin. *God has not rejected his people whom he foreknew* … As regards the gospel they are enemies of God for your sake; *but as regards election they are beloved, for the sake of their ancestors; for the gifts and the calling of God are irrevocable.* Just as you were once disobedient to God but have now received mercy because of their disobedience, so they have now been disobedient in order that, by the mercy shown to you, *they too may now receive mercy*" (11:1-2, 28-31) (italics added). According to Rokéah, *Justin Martyr and the Jews*, p. 30, Justin was very familiar with Romans.

199 O. Skarsaune, *The Proof from Prophecy*, E.J. Brill, Leiden, 1987, p. 433.

Chapter 7

Summary

Justin was a fervent apologist on behalf of the Great Church, opposing the Roman state, philosophers, heretics, popular calumnies and the Jews. In the preceding chapters, I have both outlined the various arguments employed by Justin in *1* and *2 Apologies* and *Dialogue* and analysed their appropriateness for achieving his apologetical objectives vis-à-vis the 'five-fold attack.'

In *Chapter One* we discussed how the apologists emerged in the second century to meet the challenges of the day with developed arguments and reasoned replies to the questions then being asked by the world. With respect to Justin, I asked whether his arguments were reasonable, possessing at least a potential for effectiveness having regard to both the outcomes he hoped to achieve and his audience, or if they would have been dismissed, or even worsened the plight for Christians. Justin's struggle exemplified how the apologist must adapt his arguments to the particular circumstances and challenges of the age to be effective.

In *Chapter Two* we outlined in detail the particular attacks experienced by the Christians in Justin's time. These attacks came, firstly, from the Roman state, which regarded Christianity as a threat to the established order of society and all forms of Graeco-Roman *pietas*. Christian impiety, or atheism, endangered the *pax deorum*, that is, the goodwill of the gods on which the prosperity of the empire depended. Throughout much of the second century, Christians were liable to condemnation and death for their name alone, without any other crime being proved against them. Meanwhile, philosophers directed their skill and subtlety against the uniqueness of Christ and specific articles of Christian belief, including the doctrines of creation, revelation, angels, judgement, hell, the resurrection, free will and responsibility. Other intellectual pagans employed mockery and silence. Heretics such as Simon the Magician and Marcion were the 'enemy within' and constituted a chief danger. The beliefs and practices of Judaising Christians were also of some concern, while Jewish opposition to Christianity remained strong. Justin believed that the Jews spread calumnies about the Christians, directly attacked the person of Jesus of Nazareth, and thrice-daily pronounced curses against the Christians in their synagogues. Finally, writers such as Lollianus, Fronto and later Celsus helped popularise accusations of sexual debauchery, ritual murder and cannibalism, which, whether false or not, increased the danger for all early Christians.

In *Chapter Three* we looked at Christian apology and its relationship to petitions to the Roman emperors. What features were typical of petitions presented to the emperors? Did the Christian apologists adhere to the standard requirements of form, as well as the rhetorical and literary conventions of the second century when writing to the emperors? How did Justin employ rhetoric in his apologetical writings compared to non-Christian discourses and the strategies used in rhetoric in general? Assessing the appropriateness of Justin's apologetical arguments cannot be adequately achieved without applying criteria that includes rhetorical strategies employed in the Graeco-Roman world. I concluded that Justin's apologies constituted "apologetically grounded petitions," a significant literary vehicle with no previous precedent in the Graeco-Roman literary tradition. However, they were over-lengthy compared to the standard length of petitions and thus probably intended for public display and circulation rather than for the emperors themselves. Justin's extensive use of rhetoric showed that he was both radical and independent enough to try something beyond Christian convention.

In *Chapter Four* we examined the questions of intended destination, structure and purposes of Justin's apologetical works. This examination involved an extensive review of competing scholarly opinions, after which I made the following conclusions:

(i)   Justin published his *Apologies* as open letters to the government seeking an end the arbitrary injustices committed by the Roman judicial procedure against Christians by establishing the latter's innocence in the eyes of the general public and philosophically-minded (and through them to the emperors) against the charges of atheism, immorality and disloyalty, to overcome ignorance and prejudice by showing forth Christianity's rationality through an unabridged presentation of Christian doctrines and practices and to recommend it to his pagan addressees as the only safe and useful philosophy so to ultimately win their adherence, or to at least enlist public sympathy and support for an end to arbitrary injustice, to challenge the emperors' right to their noble titles before the general public and his fellow Christians, and for the catechetical, rhetorical and apologetical formation of Christians already in the Church.

(ii)   Justin intended *Dialogue* to be read by unattached Gentiles for the purpose of converting them to Christianity, to provide a helpful internal sourcebook to assist Christians already within the fold to defend their beliefs against well-educated Jews and to convert as many of them as possible, to combat Judaising Christians who wished to foist law-keeping on Gentile Christians in Rome, and to counter Marcion and his rejection of the Torah.

In *Chapter Five* we analysed the appropriateness of Justin's apologetical arguments in *1* and *2 Apologies*. In all, Justin employed eight major arguments, namely: Behaviour, Beliefs, Due Process, Threat, Similitude, Dependence (Source), Antiquity/Fulfilled Prophecy and Miracles to achieve his four principal objectives vis-à-vis the Roman emperors and his Christian readers. The respective appropriateness/inappropriateness of each argument are summarised as follows:

(i) Behaviour

Appropriate for:
- nullifying rumours of sexual debauchery, ritual murder, cannibalism, etc., by highlighting the innocence of communal gatherings for worship.
- presenting Christianity as worthy of consideration as a superior religio-philosophical lifestyle.
- highlighting Christianity's moral value in an age of acknowledged social decline, particularly in the areas of sexual ethics and philanthropy.
- presenting Christianity as an ally against the perverse influence of the demons.
- negating the charges of political disloyalty towards the empire.

Inappropriate for:
- inferring that virtually the whole of pagan society was subject to demonic influence, including the emperors. This smacked of Christian arrogance.
- indicting the emperors (e.g., Hadrian) for their own

  sexual vices.

- employing straightforward language to describe the Christian eucharist that may have confirmed the accusation of cannibalism in the minds of the uninitiated.
- presenting aspects of Christian asceticism (e.g., virginity) that may have appeared extreme and/or anti-social.

(ii) Beliefs

Appropriate for:

- rebutting the serious charge of atheism.
- providing an exposition of Christian beliefs to bolster claims of innocence.
- substantiating the claim that both Christian behaviour and its theoretical basis were worthy of the term 'philosophy.'
- supplying Christians, particularly neophytes, with a valuable catechetical resource.

Inappropriate for:

- introducing discussion on certain doctrines that were startling, distasteful and contrary to established pagan wisdom (e.g., the resurrection of the flesh) and which were essentially unnecessary distractions.
- unduly extending the prolixity of *1 Apology*.

(iii) Due Process

Appropriate for:

- giving recognition to the emperor's reputation for piety and justice.
- exhibiting submission to the Roman judicial process.
- admitting that Christians guilty of crimes or immorality be punished without fear or favour.

Inappropriate for:

- failing to include a *modus vivendi* with the Roman authorities considering the refusal of Christians to engage in emperor-worship.
- accusing the emperors of yielding to the instigation of the demons in the promulgation and enforcement of anti-Christian laws.
- using language towards the emperors that would have appeared incredibly insolent and insulting.

(iv) Threat

Appropriate for:

- reinforcing in Justin's Christian readers the supremacy of the Christian God and his Christ over the 'divine' emperors, providing hope that those responsible for the injustices would one day face retribution and the Christian peoples achieve vindication.

Inappropriate for:

- failing to present his petition in obsequious and appealing language.
- implicating the emperors as directly responsible for the plight of Christians, thereby changing the status of Christians from appellants to accusers and judges of the emperors.
- issuing threats of hell-fire against the emperors in the name of a God they did not recognise.

(v) Similitude

Appropriate for:

- raising the intellectual profile of the Christians.
- breaking down objections to 'difficult' Christian beliefs.

- illustrating the harmony between Christian and pagan philosophical monotheism.
- rendering absurd the singling out of Christians for persecution.
- portraying Christianity as supplementing and correcting the wisdom of the ancients, not destroying such.

Inappropriate for:
- nil.

(vi) Dependence (Source)

Appropriate for:
- being consistent with the beliefs of some recognised ancients that Plato had visited Egypt.
- making Christianity philosophically respectable to his audience.
- recognising that paganism had attained a significant degree of metaphysical truth.
- employing a concept (the *Logos*) that had recognisable counterparts in the pagan philosophical tradition.
- laying the same foundation for the truths found in Christianity and paganism.
- arguing for Christianity's possession of the fullness of truth.
- undermining Christianity's alleged novelty by identifying the ancient *Logos* with Christ.

Inappropriate for:
- assuming that the teachings of the philosophers and prophets were identical when in fact they were not.
- failing to adduce demonstrable evidence that Plato actually depended on Moses.
- claiming that Socrates and others who lived according to reason were Christians, though they lived hundreds of years before Christ.

(vii) Antiquity/Fulfilled Prophecy

Appropriate for:

- satisfying the Graeco-Roman literary tradition of the day which demanded evidence of antiquity.
- putting forward Moses and Solomon who were recognised by pagans for their antiquity and wisdom.
- adducing Old Testament prophecies that were accessible and of undoubted age and venerability.
- being valued in popular pagan, philosophical and political circles, including by Marcus Aurelius.

Inappropriate for:

- laying claim to antiquity through Judaism, a culture many pagans considered perverse and disgusting.
- quoting from Hebrew/Jewish prophets who lacked credibility in the minds of pagans who did not accept the divine inspiration of the Old Testament.
- failing to provide evidence outside the Gospel accounts establishing Christ's fulfilment of prophecy.

(viii) Miracles

Appropriate for:

- sharing the Graeco-Roman notion that conceived miracles in terms of the manifestation of a superior divine power.
- being based on the 'extraordinary,' which was the most common and persuasive means of eliciting conversion in the ancient world.
- having the potential to appeal to Marcus Aurelius, who on occasions showed a willingness to acknowledge reports of miracles as credible.
- echoing the traditional philosophical critique of pagan miracles.

Inappropriate for:

- rebutting the serious charge of atheism.
- entering a 'market-place' that was already saturated with claims of purported miracles and hence sceptical about new assertions.
- failing to produce irrefutable and objectively demonstrable evidence of Christ's past miracles.
- being potentially associated with black magic and the weakness of Justin's distinguishing evidence.

In *Chapter Six* we analysed the appropriateness of Justin's apologetical arguments in *Dialogue*. In all, Justin employed four major arguments: Superiority, Fulfilled Prophecy, Miracles and True Israel to achieve his four principal objectives. The respective appropriateness/inappropriateness of each argument are summarised as follows:

(i) Superiority

Appropriate for:

- illustrating that Christianity possessed wisdom of the kind to qualify it as a philosophy.
- countering the negative attitude that many Christians held and expressed towards philosophy.
- being a starting measure to imbue Marcus Pompeius with confidence that Christianity did not totally disdain the natural wisdom of the ancients.
- contributing to the process of Christian self-definition by making sharper the contrast with Judaism.
- appealing to sophisticated Christians engaging with pagans considering monotheism and debating Jews about Jesus.
- positing another school of thought that could supply comprehensive answers to all life's questions where **existing philosophies had failed to do so.**

Inappropriate for:
- failing to supply detailed information outlining specific aspects of Christian life and worship to buttress the claim of superiority.
- appealing only to pagans already considering either Judaism or Christianity. As Justin could not point to a pool of so-called 'Christian philosophers' most other pagans within the Graeco-Roman *paideia* would have been left aghast at such a claim.
- failing to guarantee acceptance for Christianity. Having the status of a philosopher within a recognised philosophy did not ensure protection from rebuke, censure or exile.

(ii) Fulfilled Prophecy

Appropriate for:
- assisting mainstream Christians who accepted the validity of the prophets and who required powerful ammunition to promote Jesus' messianic claims in apologetical encounters with Jews.
- establishing a common ground for debate between Jews and Christians, as well as with Judaising Christians arguing for the retention of circumcision.
- allowing Christians to nuance their approach, arguing that they were not seeking to convert Jews or Judaisers to an alien worship, but rather to come to a correct view of their own religion, history and mission.
- employing allegory and typology in a way that undermined the literal value of the Torah; furthermore, every type found by Justin was an additional nail in Marcion's rejection of the Old Testament.
- using theophanies, which provided Christians with

evidence of Christ in the Old Testament as well as his divinity; in addition, Justin's theophanies provided added grounds for opposing Marcion's rejection of the Old Testament and his theological dualism.

Inappropriate for:

- proposing interpretations that would have been regarded by the sceptical as precarious, irrational and unhistorical, creating a mistrust of allegorical exegesis as an interpretative method in general.

- claiming that certain theophanies in the Old Testament were in actual fact Christophanies, an assertion that would have confused unattached Gentiles yet unfamiliar with the developing understandings of the Trinity, while Justin's clumsy language referring to Jesus as "another God" would have violently offended the strict monotheism of Judaism.

- using source material in a haphazard manner, for example, disregarding accuracy re text and authorship would have undermined Justin's credibility and reinforced suspicions of the Septuagint in the minds of Jews and Gentiles concerned enough to take time to closely examine his written claims.

(iii) Miracles

Appropriate for:

- providing evidence to rival the stories of miracle-working rabbis (such as Honi the Circle Drawer, Hanina ben Dosa and Eliezer ben Hyrcanus) that circulated from time to time in the first and second centuries AD.

- challenging the serious allegations which circulated among Jews and certain Gentiles that Jesus was a

"magician and deceiver of the people."
- stressing that, unlike pagan magicians or Jewish miracle workers, Jesus for the most part did not include material objects or prayer in his actions.
- rebutting the allegation of plagiarism by highlighting that the prophecies concerning the miracles of Christ in fact preceded the Greeks and Romans.
- providing evidence of contemporary Christian miracles (healing and exorcism) which amounted to the most objective way of reinforcing the extraordinary happenings in the life of Jesus.
- advancing the proposition that the divine authority originally held by the Jews was now in the hands of the followers of Jesus.

Inappropriate for:
- failing to provide any evidence in support of the claim that Jewish exorcists or miracle workers employed suspect fumigations and incantations "as the pagans do."
- neglecting to mention and explain Jesus' miracles involving the use of touch, sighs and saliva.
- failing to supply sufficient evidence to contradict the charges that Christ was a deceiver, such as the holiness of Christ's life, or the absence of mercenary motives.
- failing to challenge those who alleged that Christians plagiarised the miracle accounts of Jesus from pagan miracle accounts to produce hard evidence in support of their claims.

(iv) The True Israel

Appropriate for:

- giving important self-definition to the Christian community and presenting Christianity as a clear and solid alternative for unattached Gentiles.
- dividing the Law into two categories (ethical commands and ritual prescriptions), thereby enabling the following: unattached Gentiles to perceive what was essential and what was not in the Law; Gentile Christians to resist more effectively the arguments of Judaising Christians wishing to foist law-keeping on others; and Christians to continue confidently in their reverence yet non-observance of the Law in opposition to the respective claims of the Marcionites and Jews.
- providing a valuable scriptural exegesis of the Old Testament and its relation to Christ for those who were already Christian, while reinforcing the value of the Old Testament as authentic Scripture in the face of Marcionism.
- enhancing the starkness of the choice between Christianity and Judaism for unattached Gentiles— pointing out the destruction of Jerusalem and its Temple, the despoliation of Judea, and the subsequent mass diaspora of the Jews would undoubtedly have devalued the appeal of Judaism.
- proposing a 'pro-Christian' interpretation of history, that had the potential to achieve two objectives: (i) to distance Christians from the Jews while at the same time claim continuity with God's designs; (ii) to rebut the Marcionite notion that the God of the Old Testament was God of the Jews only, who was separate from and inferior to the God of the Christians.

Inappropriate for:

- asserting that the Law and its precepts were evidence of the Jewish nation's perversity rather than being a positive pedagogical gift signifying the election of Israel — circumcision was in reality a sign of union and blessing, not a sign of curse.
- employing a version of the Septuagint that contained corruptions, revisions and additions in comparison with the Hebrew Old Testament.
- failing to establish his (Justin's) credentials to interpret Scripture and to provide conclusive evidence of Jewish tampering of Scripture verses—both of which exposed his higher claim to ownership to serious ridicule.
- failing to acknowledge that in all instances of past Hebrew/Jewish infidelity there always remained a 'faithful remnant' through which God continued to work.
- the use of vituperative language, which though not entirely out of order, could have been moderated.
- omitting any reference to the 'end times' corporate conversion of the Jews which would have pre-empted and forestalled the later stigmatisation of the Jewish people.

As can be seen from the above, all of Justin's arguments were appropriate for one or more reasons, with only the argument of Threat in the *Apologies* being largely inappropriate. At the same time, all his arguments contained notable weaknesses, except for the argument of Similitude.

How has this study furthered our knowledge and understanding of Justin and his apologetical works? What can we conclude about Justin and his works based on the appropriateness or inappropriateness of his arguments? It is clear that for both the *Apologies* and *Dialogue* the strengths of Justin's arguments outweigh their weaknesses. The strengths generally pertain to philosophical, religious, or ethical aspects of the works that are presented logically and cogently while the weaknesses, by and large, result from Justin's tendency to affront his opponents. Justin wrote very much the way he lived. As a philosopher and skilled debater Justin was not above attacking those with whom he did not agree if he thought this would increase the reception of his message. His brilliance and affrontry proved to be a lethal combination and led to his ultimate silencing. It perhaps also curtailed the effectiveness of his writings, for no change of policy was ever effected during his lifetime, or at least universally implemented. Neither is there any record of positive Jewish reactions or responses to *Dialogue*. The only thing that is certain is that the memory of Justin and the influence of his writings have remained favourably preserved in the minds of Christians ever since, and will probably continue to be so favoured as long as there exists that mysterious phenomenon called Christianity.

Appendix

The Acts of the Martyrdom of *St Justin* and his Companions

By an anonymous eyewitness

THIS READING is taken from the anonymous Acts of the Martyrdom of Saint Justin and his Companion Saints written shortly after the martyrdom of St. Justin in Rome during the reign of Emperor Marcus Aurelius around the year AD 165. It is used in the Roman Liturgy's Office of Readings for the memorial of Justin Martyr, June 1.

The saints were seized and brought before the prefect of Rome, whose name was Rusticus. As they stood before the judgement seat, Rusticus the prefect said to Justin: "Above all, have faith in the gods and obey the emperors." Justin said: "We cannot be accused or condemned for obeying the commands of our Savior, Jesus Christ."

Rusticus said: "What system of teaching do you profess?" Justin said: "I have tried to learn about every system, but I have accepted the true doctrines of the Christians, though these are not approved by those who are held fast by error."

The prefect Rusticus said: "Are those doctrines approved by you, wretch that you are?" Justin said: "Yes, for I follow them with their correct teaching."

The prefect Rusticus said: "What sort of teaching is that?" Justin said: "Worship the God of the Christians. We hold him to be from the beginning the one creator and maker of the whole creation, of things seen and things unseen. We worship also the Lord Jesus Christ, the Son of God. He was foretold by the prophets as the future herald of salvation for the human race and the teacher of distinguished disciples. For myself, since I am a human being, I consider that what I say is insignificant in comparison with his infinite Godhead. I acknowledge the existence of a prophetic power, for the one I have just spoken of as the Son of God was the subject of prophecy. I know that the prophets were inspired from above when they spoke of his coming among men."

Rusticus said: "You are a Christian, then?" Justin said: "Yes, I am a Christian."

The prefect said to Justin: "You are called a learned man and think that you know what is true teaching. Listen: if you were scourged and beheaded, are you convinced that you would go up to heaven?" Justin said: "I hope that I shall enter God's house if I suffer that way. For I know that God's favour is stored up until the end of the whole world for all who have lived good lives."

The prefect Rusticus said: "Do you have an idea that you will go up to heaven to receive some suitable rewards?" Justin said: "It is not an idea that I have; it is something I know well and hold to be most certain."

The prefect Rusticus said: "Now let us come to the point at issue, which is necessary and urgent. Gather round then and with one accord offer sacrifice to the gods." Justin said: "No one who is right thinking stoops from true worship to false worship."

The prefect Rusticus said: "If you do not do as you are commanded you will be tortured without mercy." Justin said:

"We hope to suffer torment for the sake of our Lord Jesus Christ, and so be saved. For this will bring us salvation and confidence as we stand before the more terrible and universal judgement-seat of our Lord and Savior."

In the same way the other martyrs also said: "Do what you will. We are Christians; we do not offer sacrifice to idols."

The prefect Rusticus pronounced sentence, saying: "Let those who have refused to sacrifice to the gods and to obey the command of the emperor be scourged and led away to suffer capital punishment according to the ruling of the laws." Glorifying God, the holy martyrs went out to the accustomed place. They were beheaded, and so fulfilled their witness of martyrdom in confessing their faith in their Savior.

Bibliography

Primary Sources

Ante Nicene Fathers, vol. 3, ed. Alexander Roberts and James Donaldson, rev. A. Cleveland Coxe, Eerdmans, Grand Rapids, 1897, the complete works of Minucius Felix, Origen and Tertullian.

Barnard, L.W., *St. Justin Martyr: The First and Second Apologies*, Paulist Press, New York/Mahwah N.J., 1997.

Eusebius, *History of the Church*, translated by G. A. Robinson, revised by Andrew Louth, Penguin Books, Harmondsworth, Middlesex, England, 1989.

Falls, Thomas B., *St. Justin Martyr: Dialogue with Trypho*, revised by Thomas P. Halton, ed. Michael Slusser, The Catholic University of America Press, Washington D.C., 2003.

Jurgens, W. A., *The Faith of the Early Fathers*, vol. 1, The Liturgical Press, Collegeville, Minnesota, 1970.

Musurillo, H., *The Acts of the Christian Martyrs*, Clarendon Press, Oxford, 1972.

Numenius, E. des Places (ed.), Paris: Les Belles Lettres, 1973.

Pliny, *Natural History*, 28.4. Translated by W. H. S. Jones, vol. 8. The Loeb Classical Library, ed. G.P. Goold, Harvard University Press, Cambridge, Mass., 1963.

Secondary Sources

Andresen, C., "Justin und der mittlere Platonismus," *Zeitschrift für die neutestamentliche Wissenschaft* 44 (1952): 157-195.

Aune, D. E., "Magic in Early Christianity," *ANRW* II.23.2: pp. 1507-1557.

Barnard, L. W., "The Old Testament and Judaism in the Writings of Justin Martyr," *Vetus Testamentum* 14 (1964), pp. 395-406.

Barnard, L. W., *Justin Martyr – His Life and Thought*, Cambridge University Press, London, 1967.

Barnard, L. W., "The Logos Theology of St. Justin Martyr," *The Downside Review* 89 (1971), pp. 132-141.

Barnard, L. W., *St. Justin Martyr the First and Second Apologies*, Paulist Press, New York/Mahwah N.J., 1997.

Barnes, T. D., *Early Christianity in the Roman Empire*, Variorum Reprints, London, 1984.

Baus, K., *Handbook of Church History*, vol. 1: *From the Apostolic Community to Constantine*, Burns & Oates, London, 1965.

Birley, A., *Marcus Aurelius: A Biography*, rev. ed., New Haven, Yale, 1987.

Blomberg, C. L., *The Historical Reliability of the Gospels*, Inter-Varsity Press, Leicester, 1987.

Blunt, A. W. F., *The Apologies of Justin Martyr*, Cambridge University Press, London, 1911.

Bobertz, C. A., "The Role of Patron in the Cena Dominica of Hippolytus' Apostolic Tradition," *Journal of Theological Studies* 44 n.s. (1993), pp. 170-184.

Bokser, B. Z., "Justin Martyr and the Jews," *The Jewish Quarterly Review* 64 (1973), pp. 204-211.

Boyarin, D., "Justin Martyr Invents Judaism," Church History 70 (2001), pp. 427-461.

Buck, P. Lorraine, "Athenagoras's *Embassy*: A Literary Fiction," *Harvard Theological Review* 89 (1996) pp. 209-226.

Buck, P. Lorraine, "Justin Martyr's *Apologies:* Their Number, Destination, and Form," *Journal of Theological Studies*, NS, 54/1 (2003), pp. 45-59.

Campenhausen, H. von, *The Fathers of the Greek Church*, A & C Black, London, 1963.

Cary, M., *A History of Rome Down to the Reign of Constantine*, 2nd edn, MacMillan, London, 1965, 2nd edn.

Chadwick, H., "Justin Martyr's Defence of Christianity," *Bulletin of the John Rylands Library*, vol. 47, 1965, pp. 275-297.

Chadwick, H., *Early Christian Thought and the Classical Tradition: Studies in Justin, Clement, and Origen*, Clarendon Press, Oxford, 1966.

Charlesworth, M. P., "Some Observations on Ruler-Cult Especially in Rome," *Harvard*

Theological Review 28 (1935), pp. 31-42.

Cohen, J. S., *Conversion to Judaism: A History and Analysis*, Ktav., Hoboken, NJ, 1992.

Colson, F. H., "Notes and Studies," *Journal of Theological Studies* 23 (1922), pp. 161-171.

Conzelmann, H., *Gentiles, Jews, Christians: Polemics and Apologetics in the Graeco-Roman Era*, Fortress Press, Minneapolis, 1992.

Cook, J. G., "The Protreptic Power of Early Christian Language from John to Augustine," *Vigiliae Christianae* 48 (1994), pp. 105-134.

Cosgrove, H., "Justin Martyr and the Emerging Christian Canon," *Vigiliae Christianae* 36 (1982), pp. 209-232.

Cruttwell, C. T., *A Literary History of Early Christianity*, vol. 2, C. Griffin & Co., London, 1893.

Daniélou, J., *The Christian Centuries – The First Six Hundred Years*, Darton, Longman and Todd, London, 1964.

Denning-Bolle, S., "Christian Dialogue as Apologetic: The Case of Justin Martyr seen in Historical Context," *Bulletin of the John Rylands Library* 69 (1986-87), pp. 492-510.

Droge, A. J., "Justin Martyr and the Restoration of Philosophy," *Church History* 56 (1987), pp. 303-319.

Dulles, A., *A History of Apologetics*, Ignatius Press, San Francisco, 2005.

Dunn, G. D., "The Universal Spread of Christianity as a Rhetorical Argument in Tertullian's Adversus Judaeos," *Journal of Early Christian Studies* 8:1 (2000), pp. 1-19.

Dunn, G. D., *Tertullian*, Routledge, New York, 2004.

Durant, W., *Caesar and Christ: A History of Roman Civilisation and of Christianity from their beginnings to AD 325*, Simon and Schuster, New York, 1972.

Edwards, M. J., "Justin's Logos and the Word of God," *Journal of Early Christian Studies* vol. 3, no. 3 (1995), pp. 261-280.

Ehrhardt, A., "Justin Martyr's two Apologies," *Journal of Ecclesiastical History* 4 (1953-54), pp. 1-12.

Ferreiro, A, *Simon Magus in Patristic, Medieval and Early Modern Traditions*, Brill, Leiden-Boston, 2005.

Fox, R. L. *Pagans and Christians*, Knopf, New York, 1987.

Frend, W.H.C., "The Old Testament in the Age of the Greek Apologists," *Scottish Journal of Theology* 26 (1973), pp. 129-150.

Frend, W.H.C., *The Rise of Christianity*, Fortress, Philadelphia, 1984, p. 234.

Frith, F., "Saint Justin's Apologia," *Canadian Catholic Review*, 7 (Nov. 1989), pp. 394-395.

Gibbon, E., *History of the Decline and Fall of the Roman Empire*, ch. 3, J.M. Dent & Sons, London, 1966.

Goodenough, E. R., *The Theology of Justin Martyr*, Philo Press, Amsterdam, 1968.

Goodman, M., *Mission and Conversion: Proselytizing in the Religious History of the Roman Empire*, Oxford University Press, Oxford, 1994.

Grant, R. M., "The Chronology of the Greek Apologists," *Vigiliae Christianae* 9 (1955), pp. 25-33.

Grant, R. M., "The Fragments of the Greek Apologists and Irenaeus," in *Biblical and Patristic Studies in Memory of R. P. Casey*, J. N. Birdsall ed., Herder, Freiburg, 1963.

Grant, R. M., *Augustine to Constantine—The Thrust of the Christian Movement into the Roman World*, Collins, London, 1971.

Grant, R. M., *Greek Apologists of the Second Century*, SCM Press, London, 1988.

Guerra, A. J., "The Conversion of Marcus Aurelius and Justin Martyr: The Purpose, Genre, and Content of the First Apology," *The Second Century* 9 (1992), pp. 129-187.

Hamilton, J., "Justin's *Apology*, 66. A Review of Scholarship and a Suggested Synthesis," *Ephemerides Theologicae Lovanienses* XLVIII (1979), pp. 554-560.

Hardy, E. R., *Early Christian Fathers*, ed. C. C. Richardson, London, 1953.

Herr, M. D., "Persecutions and Martyrdom in Hadrian's Day," *Scripta Hierosolymitana* 23 (1972), pp. 85-125.

Hertling, L. & Kirschbaum, E., *The Roman Catacombs and their Martyrs*, Darton, Longman & Todd, London, 1960.

Holte, R., "Logos Spermatikos – Christianity and Ancient Philosophy according to St. Justin's Apologies," *Studia Theologica* 12 (1958), pp. 109-168.

Hommel, H., "Sebasmata: Studien zur antiken Religionsgeschichte und zum frühen Christentum," vol. 2, WUNT 32, Tübingen, 1984.

Horbury, W., "The Benediction of the *Minim* and Early Jewish-Christian Controversy," *Journal of Theological Studies* n.s. 33 (1982), pp. 19-61.

Horbury, W., *Jews and Christians in Contact and Controversy*, T & T Clark, Edinburgh, 1998.

Horner, T. J., "Justin's Mission to the Jews," *The Covenant Quarterly* 56/4 (1998), pp. 33-44.

Hulen, A. B., "The 'Dialogues with the Jews' as sources for the early Jewish argument against Christianity," *Journal of Biblical Literature* 51 (1932), pp. 58-70.

Janowitz, N., "Magic in the Roman Empire: Pagans, Jews, and Christians," in *Religion in the First Christian Centuries*, Routledge, New York, 2001.

Kennedy, G. A., *Classical Rhetoric and its Christian and Secular Tradition from Ancient to Modern Times*, The University of North Carolina Press, Chapel Hill, 1980.

Kennedy, G. A., *Greek Rhetoric Under Christian Emperors*, Princeton University Press, Princeton, New Jersey, 1983.

Kennedy, G. A., *New Testament Interpretation Through Rhetorical Criticism*, University of North Carolina Press, Chapel Hill, 1984.

Keresztes, P., "Law and Arbitrariness in the Persecution of the Christians and Justin's First Apology," *Vigiliae Christianae* 18 (1964), pp. 204-214.

Keresztes, P., "The Literary Genre of Justin's First Apology," *Vigiliae Christianae* 19 (1965), pp. 99-110.

Kinsig, W., "Der Sitz im Leben der Apologie in der Alten Kirche," *Zeitschrift für Kirchengeschichte* 100 (1989): pp. 291-317.

Krauss S., & Horbury, W., *The Jewish-Christian Controversy from the earliest times to 1789*, vol. 1, J. C. B. Mohr, Tübingen, 1996.

La Piana, G., "Foreign Groups in Rome during the First Centuries of the Empire," *Harvard Theological Review* 20 (1927), pp. 183-403 at p. 371.

Lieu, J. M., *Image and Reality—The Jews in the World of the Christians in the Second Century*, T & T Clark, Edinburgh, 1996.

Luck, G., *Arcana Mundi. Magic and the Occult in the Greek and Roman World*, John Hopkins University, Baltimore, 1985.

Mach, M., "Justin Martyr's *Dialogus cum Tryphone Iudaeo* and the Development of Christian Anti-Judaism," in O. Limor & G. G. Stroumsa, eds., *Contra Iudaeos: Ancient and Medieval Polemics between Christians and Jews*, J. C. B. Mohr, Tübingen, 1996, pp. 30 and 47.

Mack, B. L., *Rhetoric and the New Testament*, Guides to Biblical Scholarship, Fortress Press, Minneapolis, 1990.

MacMullen, R., *Christianizing the Roman Empire*, Yale University Press, New Haven/London, 1984.

Mair, L. P., *An Introduction to Social Anthropology*, Clarendon Press, Oxford, 1965.

Markschies, C., *Gnosis: An Introduction*, trans. by J. Bowden, T & T Clark, London and New York, 2003.

Martindale, C. C., *St. Justin the Martyr*, Harding and More, London, 1921.

Marshall, J. L., "Some observations on Justin Martyr's use of Testimonies," *Studia Patristica* 16/2 (1985), pp. 197-200.

Mason, S., "Philosophai: Graeco-Roman, Judean and Christian," in *Voluntary Associations in the Graeco-Roman World*, edd. J. S. Kloppenborg and S.G. Wilson, Routledge, London and New York, 1996, pp. 31-55.

McCready, W. O. "Ekklēsia and Voluntary Associations," in *Voluntary Associations in the Graeco-Roman World*, edd. J. S. Kloppenborg and S.G. Wilson, Routledge, London and New York, 1996, pp. 59-73.

Millar, F., *The Emperor in the Roman World: 31B.C.- A.D. 337*, Duckworth, London, 1977.

Moreau, J., *The Persecution of Christians in the Roman Empire*, Presses Universitaires de France, Paris, 1956.

Neusner, J., *Messiah in Context: Israel's History and Destiny in Formative Judaism, Part Two: Teleology*, Fortress Press, Philadelphia, 1984.

Nilson, J., "To whom is Justin's *Dialogue with Trypho* addressed?," *Journal of Theological Studies*, n.s. 38 (1977), pp. 538-546 at p. 539.

Norris, R. A., *A Study in Justin Martyr, Irenaeus, Tertullian and Origen*, Adam & Charles Black, London, 1966.

Osborn, E. F., "Justin's Response to Second Century Challenges," *Australian Biblical Review* 14 (1966), pp. 37-54.

Osborn, E. F., *Justin Martyr*, J. C. B. Mohr, Tübingen, 1973.

Osborn, E. F., "Justin Martyr and the Logos Spermatikos," *Studia Missionalia* 42 (1993), pp. 143-159.

Pagels, E., "Christian Apologists and the 'Fall of the Angels': An Attack on Roman Imperial Power," *Harvard Theological Review* 78 (1985), pp. 301-325.

Palmer, D. W., "Atheism, Apologetic, and Negative Theology in the Greek Apologists of the Second Century," *Vigiliae Christianae* 37 (1983), pp. 234-259.

Patterson, L. G., *God and History in Early Christian Thought: A Study of the Themes from Justin Martyr to Gregory the Great*, Adam & Charles Black, London, 1967.

Price, R. M., "'Hellenization' and Logos Doctrine in Justin Martyr," *Vigiliae Christianae*

42 (1988), pp. 18-23.

Price, R. M., "Are there 'Holy Pagans' in Justin Martyr?," *Studia Patristica* 31 (1997), pp. 167-171.

Pryor, J. W., "Justin Martyr and the Fourth Gospel," *The Second Century* 9, 3 (1992), pp. 153-169.

Purves, G. T., *The Testimony of Justin Martyr to Early Christianity*, J. Nisbet, London, 1888.

Quasten, J., *Patrology*, vol. 1, *The Beginnings of Patristic Literature*, The Newman Press, Maryland, 1950.

Räisänen, H., "Marcion," in *A Companion to Second-Century Christian "Heretics,"* Edd. A. Marjanen & P. Luomanen, Brill, Leiden, 2005, pp. 100-122.

Rajak, T., "Talking at Trypho: Christian Apologetic as Anti-Judaism in Justin's *Dialogue with Trypho the Jew*," in *Apologetics in the Roman Empire: Pagans, Jews and Christians*, edd. M. Edwards, M. Goodman & S. Price, Oxford University Press, 1999, pp. 59-80.

Remus, H., "Magic or Miracle? Some Second-Century Instances," *The Second Century* 2, 3 (1982), pp. 127-156.

Remus, H., *Pagan-Christian Conflict over Miracle in the Second Century*, The Philadelphia Patristic Foundation, Philadelphia, 1983.

Remus, H., "Justin Martyr's Argument with Judaism," in *Anti-Judaism in Early Christianity*, vol. 2: *Separation and Polemic*, Stephen G. Wilson, ed., Wilfrid Laurier University Press, Waterloo, Ontario, 1986, pp. 59-80.

Rexine, John E., "Daimon in Classical Greek Literature," *Greek Orthodox Theological Review*, 30 (1985), pp. 335-361.

Rhee, H., *Early Christian Literature: Christ and Culture in the Second and Third Centuries*, Routledge, London and New York, 2005.

Rokéah, D., *Jews, Pagans and Christians in Conflict*, The Magnes Press, Jerusalem, 1982.

Rokéah, D., *Justin Martyr and the Jews*, Brill, Leiden, 2002.

Romanides, J. S., "Justin Martyr and the Fourth Gospel," *The Greek Orthodox Theological Review* 4 (1958-1959), pp. 115-134.

Schoedel, W., "Apologetic Literature and Ambassadorial Activities," *Harvard Theological Review* 82 (1989), pp. 55-78 at 57.

Schönborn, C., "Does the Church Need Philosophy?," *Communio* 15 (1988), pp. 334-

349.

Setzer, C. J., *Jewish Responses to Early Christians, History and Polemics, 30-150 CE*, Fortress Press, Minneapolis, 1994.

Shotwell, W. A., *The Biblical Exegesis of Justin Martyr*, S.P.C.K., London, 1965.

Sikora, J. J., "Philosophy and Christian Wisdom According to Saint Justin Martyr," *Franciscan Studies* 23/1 (1963-4), pp. 244-256.

Skarsaune, O., "The Conversion of Justin Martyr," *Studia Theologica* 30 (1976), pp- 53-73.

Skarsaune, O., *The Proof from Prophecy*, E.J. Brill, Leiden, 1987.

Smith, M. *Tannaitic Parallels to the Gospels*, Society of Biblical Literature, Philadelphia, 1951.

Stanton, G. N., "Aspects of Early Christian-Jewish Polemic and Apologetic," *New Testament Studies* 31 (1985), pp. 377-392.

Stanton, G. N., "Justin Martyr's Dialogue with Trypho: group boundaries, 'proselytes' and 'God-fearers,'" in *Tolerance and Intolerance in Early Judaism and Christianity*, Cambridge University Press, 1998.

St. Croix, G.E.M. de, "The Persecutions," in *The Crucible of Christianity*, Arnold Toynbee, ed., Thames and Hudson, London, 1969.

Stroumsa, G., "From Anti-Judaism to Antisemitism in Early Christianity?" in O. Limor and G. G. Stroumsa (eds), *Contra Iudaeos: Ancient and Medieval Polemics between Christians and Jews*, Texts and Studies in Medieval and Early Modern Judaism 10. Tübingen: J. C. B. Mohr, 1996, pp. 1-26.

Stylianopoulos, T., *Justin Martyr and the Mosaic Law*, Society of Biblical Literature, Missoula, 1975.

Theissen, G., *The Miracle Stories of the Early Christian Tradition*, Fortress Press, Philadelphia, 1983.

Thornton, T. C. G., "Christian Understandings of the *Birkath-Ha-Minim* in the Eastern Roman Empire," *Journal of Theological Studies* n.s. 38 (1987), pp. 419-431.

Wagner, W. H., *Christianity in the Second Century – After the Apostles*, Fortress Press, Minneapolis, 1994.

Wehofer, Th., *Die Apologie Justins des Philosopher und Märtyrers in literarhistorischer Beziehung zum erstenmal untersucht* (Römische Quartalschrift, Suppl. 6, 1897).

Wilder, A. N., *Early Christian Rhetoric: The Language of the Gospel*, Hendrickson, Peabody,

Massachusetts, 1964.

Wilken, R. L., "Toward a Social Interpretation of Early Christian Apologetics," *Church History* 39 (1970), pp. 437-458.

Wilken, R. L., *The Spirit of Early Christian Thought*, Yale University Press, New Haven and London, 2003.

Williams, M. A., *Rethinking "Gnosticism": An Argument for Dismantling a Dubious Category*, Princeton University Press, Princeton, 1996.

Wilson, S. G., *Related Strangers: Jews and Christians 70-170 CE*, Fortress Press, Minneapolis, 1995.

Wilson, S. G., "Voluntary Associations: An Overview," in *Voluntary Associations in the Graeco-Roman World*, edd. J. S. Kloppenborg and S.G. Wilson, Routledge, London and New York, 1996, pp. 1- 15.

Winden, J. C. M. van, *An Early Christian Philosopher – Justin Martyr's Dialogue with Trypho Chapters One to Nine*, E. J. Brill, Leiden, 1971.

Wooten, C. W., "The Ambassador's Speech: A Particular Hellenistic Genre of Oratory," *Quarterly Journal of Speech* 59 (1973), pp. 209-212.

Young, F., "Greek Apologists of the Second Century," in *Apologetics in the Roman Empire: Pagans, Jews and Christians*, edd. M. Edwards, M. Goodman & S. Price, Oxford University Press, Oxford, 1999.

Young, M. O., "Justin, Socrates and the Middle-Platonists," *Studia Patristica* 18/2 (1989), pp. 161-165.

www.ingramcontent.com/pod-product-compliance
Lightning Source LLC
Chambersburg PA
CBHW022144050726
47590CB00002B/585